W9-AZX-836

The 7-Day Afghan Book

Revised Edition

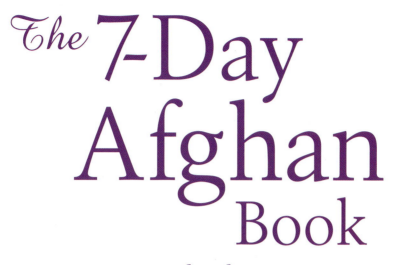

by Jean Leinhauser and Rita Weiss

Sterling Publishing Co., Inc.
New York

Library of Congress Cataloging-in-Publication Data

Published by Sterling Publishing Co., Inc.
387 Park Avenue South, New York, NY 10016
© 1985 by Jean Leinhauser and Rita Weiss
© 2004 by The Creative Partners, LLC™
Distributed in Canada by Sterling Publishing
C/o Canadian Manda Group, 165 Dufferin Street
Toronto, Ontario, Canada M6K 3H6
Distributed in Great Britain by Chrysalis Books Group PLC
The Chrysalis Building, Bramley Road, London W10 6SP, England
Distributed in Australia by Capricorn Link (Australia) Pty. Ltd.
P.O. Box 704, Windsor, NSW 2756, Australia

Printed in the USA
All rights reserved

Sterling ISBN 1-4027-1378-9

Introduction

Whether we crochet or knit afghans for ourselves, for gifts, or as donations to a good cause, most of us like to make them in a hurry. Perhaps that's why *The 7-Day Afghan Book*, which we wrote in 1985, has remained in print and become a classic.

Times change. We still like to make afghans quickly, but our tastes in color and style are now different. That's why when our publisher suggested updating the book for a new edition, we jumped at the chance to bring our afghans into the twenty-first century.

We reviewed the projects in the original book and found that most of the yarns we had used were no longer being made. We decided to re-work those afghans in the new yarns and the new colors. We also added afghans made with the wonderful new yarns on the market today. We found some afghan designs that might have been popular in the eighties certainly wouldn't fit into our modern life styles. So we deleted some designs and added some new ones.

As we said in the introduction to our original edition, these afghans can be made in a week—but that, of course, depends on how many hours you're planning to spend with your crochet hook or your knitting needles, and how fast you work. Knitting and crocheting should not be a race; there's no prize for the one who gets there first! Take time and enjoy your work, relax, have fun. Don't feel you're up against the clock or the calendar just because we've called this *The 7-Day Afghan Book*.

And, by the way, if you can't remember how to make an afghan, or if you're stymied by all of those abbreviations and symbols, we've included a section on Afghan Basics, starting on page 137.

Going through the afghans was like a trip back in time for us. We may be older now, but we still love to make afghans, and we hope you do too—especially when you can make one in just one week.

Jean Leinhauser   *Rita Weiss*

Flower Field Lapghan
6

Ice Crystals
9

Beautiful in Blue Cables
13

Orchid Lace
16

Rosy Ripple
18

Fantastic Fisherman
21

Watercolors Afghan
24

Raspberry Rose
27

Summer Garden
30

Quick Lace
33

Multi-Color Striped
36

Marvelous Mauve Lapghan
39

Blue Lagoon
42

Peppermint Candy Baby Afghan
45

Vanilla Lace Throw
48

In the Pink
50

Easy Feather and Fan
52

Blue Rhapsody
54

Pink Petals
57

Stripes on Parade
59

Lovely Lace
62

Raspberries and Cream
65

Delightful Daisies
68

Pretty Stripes
71

Rosy Future
74

Roses in the Snow
77

Feather and Fan
80

Ocean Waves
82

Rippling Shells
85

Plum Pretty
88

Summer Skies
90

Beautiful Bobbles
94

Sweet Cream
97

Diagonal Chevrons
100

Perfect Plaid
104

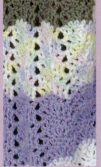

Sedona Rocks
107

Just for Fun
110

Fisherman Cables and Lattice
113

Horseshoe Cables
117

Coral Seas Throw
120

Mock Fisherman
122

Blue Boy
125

Gingham and Lace
128

Classic Granny
131

Dimensional Shells
134

Afghan Basics
137

Flower Field Lapghan

What a pretty way to keep warm! The always-favorite color combination of rose and white creates a lapghan that you'll love to use. This is also a perfect gift for a friend, using her own décor colors.

Size
28" x 32"

Materials
Worsted weight yarn:
6 oz white
12 oz rose

(Photographed afghan made in Caron® Simply Soft® Colors #9701 White and #9721 Victorian Rose)

Size H (5 mm) crochet hook (or size required for gauge)

Gauge
One square = $3^3/4$"

Instructions

Granny Square (make 56)

With rose, ch 4, join with a sl st to form a ring.

Rnd 1: Ch 1, 8 sc in ring, join to beg sc.

Rnd 2: Ch 3; in same sc, (YO, draw up a lp) twice, YO and draw through all 5 lps on hook: beg cluster made; * ch 3; in next sc, (YO, draw up a lp) 3 times, YO and draw through all 7 lps on hook: cluster made; rep from * around, ch 3, join with a sl st to top of beg ch-3; finish off rose.

continued on the next page

Flower Field Lapghan

Rnd 3: Join white in any ch-3 sp; for beg corner, ch 3, 4 dc in same sp; * 4 dc in next ch-3 sp, 5 dc in next ch-3 sp for next corner; rep from * twice more, 4 dc in next ch-3 sp, join with a sl st to top of beg ch-3; finish off-white.

Rnd 4: Join rose in top of center dc of any 5-dc corner group; ch 3, 4 dc in same st; * dc in each st to center dc of next 5-dc corner group; 5 dc in center st; rep from * twice more, dc in each st around, join; finish off.

Joining

To join, hold two squares with right sides together and with rose , sew through back loops only, carefully matching stitches. Join squares in 7 rows of 8 squares each.

Edging

Hold afghan with right side facing you.

Rnd 1: Join white with a sl st in center st of 5-dc group at any outer corner of afghan; ch 3, 4 dc in same st; dc in each dc and in each joining between squares to center st of 5-dc group at next corner, work 5 dc in center st; continue in this manner around to beg, join; finish off-white.

Rnd 2: Join rose with a sl st in center dc of 5-dc group at any corner; 3 sc in this st, sc in each dc to center st of 5-dc group at next corner; continue in this manner around to beg, join with a sl st to beg sc.

Rnd 3: Ch 1, reverse single crochet in each st around (see page 140) join, finish off and weave in ends.

Ice Crystals

Let it snow, let it snow, let it snow! You'll be beautifully warm with this striking design of frosty white ice crystals against a shimmering blue background. Two different motifs are combined to create the design.

Ice Crystals

Size

42" x 72" before fringing

Materials

Worsted weight yarn:
36 oz blue
l8 oz white

(Photographed model made with
Carion® Simply Soft® Colors #9709 Lt.
Country Blue and #9701 White)

Size G (4 mm) crochet hook (or size
required for gauge)

Gauge

Each Motif = 6" from side edge to side
edge

Instructions

Solid Motif (make 68)

Rnd 1 (right side): With blue ch 6; in 6th ch from hook work (dc, ch 3) 5 times; join with a sl st to 3rd ch of beg ch: 6 dc and 6 ch-3 spaces.

Rnd 2: Sl st into first sp, ch 3 (counts as first dc), 2 dc in same sp, ch 3; (3 dc in next sp, ch 3) 5 times, join.

Rnd 3: Ch 4 (counts as first tr); 1 tr in each of next 2 dc; * (2 tr, ch 3, 2 tr) all in next ch-3 sp; 1 tr in each of next 3 dc; rep from * 4 times more, end with (2 tr, ch 3, 2 tr) all in last ch-3 sp; join with sl st in 4th ch of beg ch: 7 dc on each side with ch-3 sp between.

Rnd 4: Ch 4 (counts as first dc and ch-1 sp); (skip 1 st, dc in tr, ch 1) twice; * (1 dc, ch 3, 1 dc) all in ch-3 sp for corner; ch 1, dc in next tr; (ch 1, skip 1 st, dc in next tr) 3 times, ch 1; rep from * 4 times more; dc in next tr, ch 1, skip last tr, join with sl st in 3rd ch of starting chain; you should have 6 dc and 5 ch-1 sps on each side between ch-3 corner sps; finish off. Weave in yarn ends.

Ice Crystal Motifs (make 36)

Rnd 1: With white ch 6; in 6th ch from hook work (dc, ch 3) 5 times; join with sl st in 3rd ch of beg ch: 6 dc and 6 ch-3 spaces.

Rnd 2: Sl st into first sp, ch 1; * (hdc, dc) in same sp; ch 6, sl st in 3rd ch from hook and in each of rem 3 ch for long picot; (dc,hdc) in same sp, ch 5; sl st in 3rd ch from hook for short picot, ch 2; rep from * in each of rem 5 sps; join in first hdc: 6 long picots and 6 short picots; finish off-white.

Rnd 3: Join blue with sl st in top of any short picot, ch 1; * sc in top of short picot, at base of next long picot work 1 tr in first hdc, 2 tr in dc, ch 1, sl st in top of long picot, ch 1; on other side of same picot work 2 tr in dc, 1 tr in hdc; rep from * 5 times more, join with sl st in first sc.

Rnd 4: Sl st into first tr, ch 4 (counts as first dc and ch-1 sp); skip 1 st, dc in next tr, ch 1; * for corner work (dc, ch 3, dc) all in sl st at top of long picot; ch 1, dc in next tr, (ch 1, skip 1 st, dc in next tr) 3 times, ch 1; rep from * 4 times more, end with (dc, ch 3, dc) all in sl st at top of last long picot, ch 1, dc in next tr, ch 1, skip 1 st, dc in next tr, ch 1, join with sl st in 3rd ch of beg ch: 6 dc and 5 ch-1 sps on each side between ch-3 corner sps; finish off, weave in yarn ends.

continued on the next page

Ice Crystals

Joining

Arrange motifs as shown in Assembly Diagram. Working from the right side of each motif with care to keep seams flat, use a yarn needle and blue to sew motifs tog with an overhand st through the back lps only of corresponding sts.

Edging

From right side, join blue with a sl st in any ch-3 corner sp on outside edge; ch 1, work 3 sc in each outer corner sp, 1 sc in each dc and in each ch-1 sp along edge of motif to last dc before joining seam; draw up a lp in each inner corner sp on both sides of seam, YO and through all 3 lps on hook for dec; continue all around outside edge in same way, join with sl st in first sc and fasten off.

Fringe

Using white, cut two lengths for fringe: 14" strands for longer panels, 20" strands for shorter panels. Following Single Knot Fringe instructions on page 140, use 4 strands doubled for each knot. Tie one knot in each of 7 spaces across lower edge of each motif on both short ends.

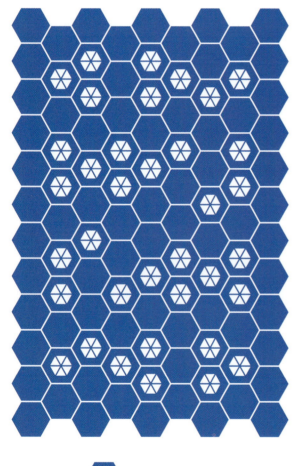

 Crystal Motif

Beautiful in Blue Cables

Two beautiful shades of blue are combined with creamy natural to create this quiet afghan, sure to provide peaceful dreams as you rest. It's easy to work in panels.

Beautiful in Blue Cables

Size

39" x 50" before fringing

Materials

Worsted weight yarn:

12 oz medium blue

6 oz natural

18 oz light blue

(Photographed model made with Bernat® Berella® "4"® Colors #08721 Medium Country Blue, #08940 Natural, and #08720 Light Country Blue)

14" size 10 (6 mm) straight knitting needles (or size required for gauge)

Size G (4 mm) aluminum crochet hook for joining panels

Cable stitch holder or double point needle

Gauge

20 sts = 3³/₄"

Note

A YO lp begins every row; for ease in counting lps and assembling panels, tie a marker of contrasting yarn every 25th lp on each side of panel. Mark cast-on row of each panel as panel bottom.

Instructions

Light Blue Panel (make 4)

With light blue, cast on 20 sts.

Row 1: YO, K 7, K 2 tog, K 11.

Rep Row 1 until there are 150 YO loops on each side of the panel. Bind off loosely.

Cable Panel (make 2 in medium blue; make 1 in natural)

Cast on 41 sts.

Row 1 (cable twist row): YO, K 7, K 2 tog, K 2; sl next 4 sts onto cable needle and hold in back of work; K 4, K 4 sts from cable needle, K 3, sl 4 sts onto cable needle and hold in back of work; K 4, K 4 sts from cable needle, K 11.

Row 2: YO, K 7. K 2 tog; K 2, P 8, K 3; P 8, K 11.

Row 3: YO, K 7, K 2 tog, K 32.

Rows 4 through 9: Rep Rows 2 and 3, 3 more times.

Row 10: Rep Row 2.

Rep these 10 rows until there are 150 YO loops on each side of the panel, ending by working Row 10.

Bind-Off Row: Bind off 7 sts; K 2 tog, bind off the K 2 tog; * place next 4 sts on cable needle, bind off 4 sts; bind off 4 sts on cable needle; bind off 3 sts; rep from * to last 11 sts, bind off.

Joining

Join panels with crochet hook, as follows: Place natural cable panel with wrong side facing wrong side of a lt blue panel and cast-on rows at bottom; join natural yarn with an sc working through both bottom YO loops; continue working sc to join YO loops, adjusting tension to keep work flat. Work to top of panels, finish off. Join another lt blue panel to other side of natural panel in same manner. Using medium blue yarn, join a medium blue panel to each of the joined lt blue panels, in same manner. Then using medium yarn, join remaining lt blue panels, one to each side of medium blue panels. Weave in all loose ends.

Fringe

Follow Single Knot Fringe instructions on page 140. Cut strands 16" long in all colors. Working across each short end of afghan, knot 1 strand in each st across, matching fringe color to panel color.

Orchid Lace

*W*hat could be easier than this 4-row pattern? And on a size 11 needle, it's fast, too. The pretty rippling effect has a lacey look you'll love.

Size

42" x 54" before fringing

Materials

Worsted weight yarn:
24 oz orchid

(Photographed model made with Caron® Simply Soft® Color #9717 Orchid)

36" size 11 (8 mm) circular needle (or size required for gauge)

Gauge

22 sts = 7"
8 rows = 2 1/2"

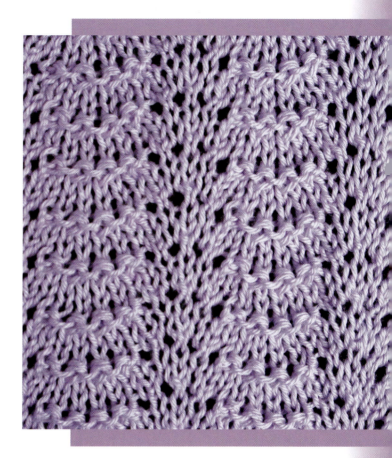

Instructions

Cast on 143 sts; do not join, work back and forth in rows.

Row 1 (right side): Knit.

Row 2: Purl.

Row 3: * (P 2 tog) twice; (inc 1, K 1) 3 times [to inc, pick up horizontal bar before next st]; inc 1, (P 2 tog) twice; rep from * across.

Row 4: Purl.

Rep these 4 rows for pattern until afghan measures 54", ending by working Row 4. Bind off in purl st.

Fringe

Follow Single Knot Fringe Instructions on page 140. Cut strands 16" and use one strand for each knot. Tie knot through every other stitch across each short end of afghan.

Rosy Ripple

This is a very easy ripple, worked with a large hook in a pattern that is just a one-row repeat. We made it in four shades or rose, accented with off-white, for a very feminine look. With just a change of color theme, it will be perfect for anyone or for any décor.

Size

42" x 62"

Materials

Worsted weight yarn:
10 oz each of burgundy (Color A)
medium rose (Color B)
light rose (Color C)
pale rose (Color D)
off-white (Color E)

(Photographed model made with Bernat® Berella® "4"® Colors #01405 Dark Burgundy (A); #08816 Medium Antique Rose (B); #08815 Antique Rose (C); #08814 Pale Antique Rose (D); and #08940 Natural (E))

Size K (6.5 mm) crochet hook (or size required for gauge)

Gauge

In pattern stitch, 2 shells = 1 1/2"

continued on the next page

Rosy Ripple

Instructions

With Color A, ch 342 LOOSELY.

Foundation Row 1: Sc in 2nd ch from hook; sk one ch, (sc, ch 2, sc) in next ch (shell made); (sk 2 ch, shell in next ch) 4 times; * sk 2 ch, (shell, ch 3, shell) all in next ch for point; (sk 2 ch, shell in next ch) 4 times; sk 2 ch, sc in next ch; sk 3 ch, sc in next ch; (sk 2 ch, shell in next ch) 4 times; rep from * 8 times more. Sk 2 ch, (shell, ch 3, shell) in next ch for last point; (sk 2 ch, shell in next ch) 5 times; sk one ch, dc in last ch.

Pattern Row : Ch 1, turn; sc in dc, sc in ch-2 sp of first shell; work shell in ch-2 sp in each of next 5 shells; * (shell, ch 3, shell) in ch-3 sp at point; shell in ch-2 sp in each of next 4 shells; sc in ch-2 sp of next shell, sk 2 sc, sc in ch-2 sp of next shell; shell in ch-2 sp in each of next 4 shells; rep from * to last point. Work (shell, ch 3, shell) in ch-3 sp at last point, shell in ch-2 sp in each of next 5 shells; sc in ch-2 sp of last shell, dc in last sc.

Rep Pattern Row in the following color sequence:

2 rows Color B

2 rows Color C

2 rows Color D

2 Rows Color E

2 Rows Color A

Note

To change colors, work last dc of row until 2 lps rem on hook; with new color, YO, draw through both lps on hook; cut old color.

Leave 4" yarn ends when starting and ending colors for weaving in later or working over on following row.

Rep 10-row color sequence, 7 more times. Finish off; weave in all ends.

Fantastic Fisherman

Fringe-as-you-go speeds the work on this sculptured beauty; there are no ends to weave in, no separate fringe to make.

Fantastic Fisherman

Size
35" x 50"

Materials
Worsted weight yarn:
30 oz off-white

(Photographed model made with Caron®
Simply Soft® Color #9702 off-white)

Size J (6 mm) crochet hook (or size
required for gauge)

Gauge
11 sc = 4"
3 sc rows = 1"

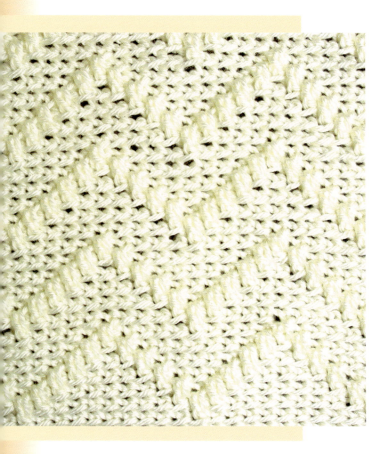

Notes

This is an unusual afghan; you make the
fringe as you work, by leaving a 7" end
of yarn at the beginning and end of
each row. The afghan is worked entirely
from the front side, so be sure never to
turn the work. Here are some techniques you will want to refer to as you
work:

1. All sc stitches are worked in the back
lp only of each stitch. This is the lp away
from you.

2. All dc stitches are worked in the front
lp of the sc stitch in the second row
below.

3. From Row 2 on, begin every row like
this: Leaving a 7" end of yarn, make a
slip knot on hook; remove hook, insert
it in first st of previous row, put slip knot
back on hook and pull lp through, ch 1.
This counts as first st of the row. This
method gives a firm selvage edge.

4. To end each row, after working last
st, cut yarn 7" from hook, pull yarn end
through lp to fasten off.

Remember that each row is worked
from the front; and that the yarn starts
and ends on each row.

Instructions

Make a slip knot on hook, leaving a 7" end; ch 167 loosely.

Row 1: Sc in 2nd ch from hook and in each ch across: 166 sc; finish off, leaving a 7" end.

Rows 2 and 3: Join yarn in first st (Note 3 above); sc in back lp only of each st across; finish off yarn (Note 4 above). Joining and ending methods will not be mentioned again.

Row 4: Join yarn in first sc, sc in next 7 sc; sk next sc, work dc in front lp of sc 2 rows below; * sc in next 9 sc; sk next sc, dc as before in 2nd row below; rep from * across, ending sc in last 7 sc; there should be 16 dc across row.

Row 5: Join yarn in first sc, sc in next 6 sc, sk next sc, dc as before; sc in next sc, sk next sc, dc as before; * 7 sc, sk next sc, dc as before, sc in next sc, sk next sc, dc as before; rep from * across, ending sc in last 6 sc; there should be 32 dc across row.

Note

From now on, remember to work each dc in front loop of sc 2 rows below skipped dc; this will not be mentioned again.

Row 6: Join yarn in first sc, sc in next 5 sc, sk next sc, dc; 3 sc, sk next sc, dc; * 5 sc, sk next sc, dc; 3 sc, sk next sc, dc; rep from * across , ending sc in last 5 sc.

Row 7: Join yarn in first sc; sc in next 4 sc, sk next sc, dc; 5 sc, sk next sc, dc; * 3 sc, sk next sc. dc, 5 sc; sk next sc, dc; rep from * across, ending sc in last 4 sc.

Row 8: Join yarn in first sc; sc in next 3 sc, sk next sc, dc; 7 sc, sk next sc, dc; * sc, sk next sc, dc; 7 sc, sk next sc, dc; rep from * across, ending sc in last 3 sc.

Row 9: Join yarn in first sc; sc in next 2 sc, sk next sc, dc; * 9 sc, sk next sc, dc; repeat from * across, ending sc in last 2 sc.

Rep Rows 4 through 9, 17 more times.

Rep Row 2, twice. Fasten off.

Edging

With right side of afghan facing and working over the row just completed, attach yarn; ch 1, sc in each stitch across. Finish off.

With right side of afghan facing and working over chain row, attach yarn, ch 1, sc in each ch across. Finish off. Trim fringe evenly.

Watercolors Afghan

*F*un to make cross stitches add definition and texture to a romantic afghan, which combines an ombre with a solid color. You could also use two solid colors, or make it entirely in one solid shade.

Size

47" x 66" before fringing

Materials

Worsted weight yarn:
33 oz ombre (Color A)
9 oz solid (Color B)

(Photographed model made with TLC® Amoré™ Color #3995, Lagoon Print (A) and #3823, Lake Blue (B))

Size J (6 mm) aluminum crochet hook (or size required for gauge)

Gauge

5 dc = 2"
3 dc rows = 2"

Note

When changing colors, YO, draw up a lp in last stitch (3 lps on hook) YO, draw through 2 lps; CHANGE TO NEW COLOR, YO, draw through rem lps.

continued on the next page

Watercolors Afghan

Instructions

With Color B, ch 119 loosely.

Row 1: Dc in 3rd ch from hook and in each rem ch: 118 dc (counting beg skipped chs as a dc); ch 2 (counts as first dc of following row throughout pattern), turn.

Row 2: Dc in each dc across and in ch-2 turning ch; ch 2, turn.

Rows 3 through 6: Rep Row 2, attach Color A on last st of Row 6; ch 2, turn.

Rows 7 through 16: Rep Row 2 in Color A for 10 rows, attach Color B on last stitch of Row 16; ch 2, turn.

Row 17: With Color B, * sk next dc, dc in next dc, dc in skipped dc: cross stitch made; rep from * across, dc in turning ch; ch 2, turn.

Row 18: Rep Row 17.

Row 19: Rep Row 17, changing to Color A on last st; ch 2, turn.

Rep Rows 7 through 19, 5 times. Rep Rows 7 through 16 one more time. Change to Color B, work 6 rows in dc. Fasten off.

Fringe

Follow Single Knot Fringe Instructions on page 140. With Color A, cut strands 16" in length. Working across each short end of afghan, using 2 strands, folded in half, make a knot in each stitch across.

Raspberry Rose

This pretty pastel afghan combines two colors with two patterns: panels of stockinette stitch with panels of lacey, open stitches. It's light-weight and soft, a pleasure to knit and to use.

Raspberry Rose

Size
48" x 53" before fringing

Materials
Worsted weight yarn:
12 oz raspberry (Color A)
12 oz rose (Color B)

(Photographed model made with Caron®
Simply Soft® Color, #2678 Soft
Raspberry (A) and Color #2661,
Victorian Rose (B))

36" size 11 (8 mm) circular needle (or
size required for gauge)

Gauge
In Stockinette Stitch (K 1 row, P 1 row):
12 sts = 4"

Note
Circular needle is used to accommodate
large number of stitches; do not join;
turn work at end of each row.

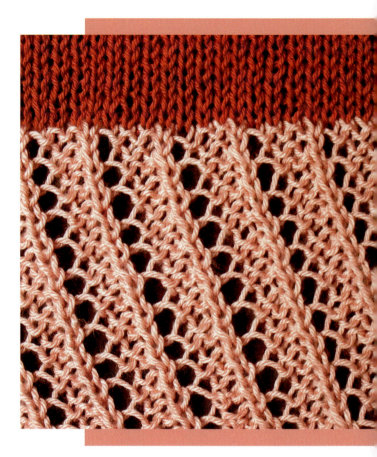

Instructions
With Color A, cast on 158 sts loosely;
afghan is worked lengthwise.

Row 1 (right side): * K 1 P 1; rep from
* across.

Row 2: Rep row 1.

These two rows create a Seed Stitch
pattern.

Rows 3 through 10: Rep Rows 1 and 2, 4 times.

** Row 11: Knit.

Row 12: Purl.

These two rows create a Stockinette Stitch pattern.

Rows 13 through 26: Rep Rows 11 and 12.

Row 27: Knit; finish off Color A.

Lace Pattern
Join Color B.

Row 1 (wrong side): Purl.

Row 2: K 1, * YO, sl 1, K 1, PSSO, P 2; repeat from * across, ending K 1.

Row 3: K 3, * P 1, K 3; repeat from * across, ending with P 1, K 2.

Row 4: K 1, P 1; * YO, sl 1, K 1, PSSO, P 2; repeat from * across, ending last rep with P 1, K 1.

Row 5: K 2, * P 1, K 3; rep from * across.

Row 6: K 1, P 2; * YO, sl 1, K 1, PSSO, P 2; rep from * across ending with YO, sl 1, K 1, PSSO, K 1.

Row 7: K 1, * P 1, K 3; rep from * across ending K 1.

Row 8: K 1, P 3, * YO, sl 1, K 1, PSSO, P 2; rep from * across ending YO, sl 1, K 1, PSSO.

Row 9: K 4, * P 1, K 3; rep from * across ending P 1, K 5.

Rep Rows 2 through 9, 2 more times for pattern. ** Repeat between ** 3 more times. Finish off Color B.

Join Color A, and work in Stockinette Stitch pattern for 17 rows. Work in Seed Stitch pattern for 10 rows. Bind off loosely in Seed Stitch.

Fringe
Follow Single Knot Fringe Instructions on page 140. Cut strands, in both colors, 16" long, and use 2 strands folded in half for each knot. Knot through every other stitch across each short end of afghan (9 knots for each Color A panel and 10 knots for each Color B panel). Repeat for other side.

Summer Garden

*F*resh summer colors create this sweet afghan, worked in an unusual pattern stitch. It's fun to make, and you can of course vary the color combinations.

Size
44" x 68"

Materials
Worsted weight yarn:
18 oz plum
18 oz celery
18 oz rose

(Photographed model made in TLC® Amoré™ Colors #3534 Plum; #3625 Celery and #3710 Rose.)

Size I (5.5 mm) crochet hook (or size required for gauge)

Gauge
11 sc = 4"

continued on the next page

Summer Garden

Instructions

Border

With plum, ch 122.

Row 1: Sc in 2nd ch from hook and in each ch across: 121 sc; ch 1, turn.

Rows 2 and 3: Sc across, ch 1, turn.

Row 4: Sc to last sc, change to celery in last st, ch 1, turn. Finish off plum.

Pattern Rows

Note

In Row 1, some single crochet sts are worked at base of sts 2 or 3 rows below; this gives a decorative shell effect.

Row 1: Sc in first sc; * sc at base of next sc; sc at base of next sc **2 rows below,** sc at base of next sc **3 rows below,** sc at base of next sc **2 rows below,** sc at base of next sc; sc in next sc; rep from * across, ending sc in last sc, ch 1, turn.

Rows 2, 3 and 4: Sc in each sc across, ch 1, turn; at end of Row 4, change to plum, finish off celery.

Rep Pattern Rows 1 through 4, changing to rose at end of Row 4.

Repeat Pattern Rows 1 through 4, changing colors in sequence, plum, celery, rose, 23 times; finish off, weave in all loose ends.

Quick Lace

This beautiful, snowy white lace afghan is knitted with two strands of yarn, on Size 15 needles – what could be faster? And you'll love the pretty, feminine look.

Quick Lace

Size
47" x 75"

Materials:
Worsted weight yarn:
40 oz white

(Photographed model made with TLC®
Amoré™, Color #3001, White)

36" size 15 (10 mm) circular needle (or
size required for gauge)

Gauge
In Stockinette St (K 1 row, P 1 row),
with 2 strands of yarn held together:
10 sts = 4"

Notes

1. Work with 2 strands of yarn held
together throughout.

2. Circular needle is used to accommodate large number of stitches; do not
join, work back and forth in rows.

Instructions
Starting at narrow edge, with 2 strands held
together cast on 116 sts. Do not join.

Row 1: YO; sl 1, K 2 tog, PSSO; * YO, K 1,
YO; sl 1, K 2 tog, PSSO; rep from * across
to within last st, YO, K 1.

Note
Be careful not to drop the YO at beg of
rows.

Row 2: YO, P across: 117 sts.

Row 3: YO, K 2 tog; * YO; sl 1, K 2 tog, PSSO; YO, K 1; rep from * across, end with YO, sl 1, K 2 tog, PSSO: 116 sts.

Row 4: Purl.

Rows 5-36: Rep Rows 1-4, eight times.

Row 37: Work first and last 12 sts as on Row 1, knit center 92 sts, working as follows: YO, sl 1, K 2 tog, PSSO (YO, K 1, YO, sl 1, K 2 tog, PSSO) twice, YO, K 1, K center 92 sts, YO, sl 1, K 2 tog, PSSO (YO, K 1, YO, Sl 1, K 2 tog, PSSO) twice, YO, K 1.

Row 38: YO, purl across.

Row 39: YO, K 2 tog; (YO; sl 1, K 2 tog, PSSO; YO, K 1) twice; YO, K 2 tog, K to last 12 sts, work in pattern across last 12 sts.

Row 40: Purl.

Rows 41-52: Rep Rows 37-40, three more times.

Row 53: Work in pattern across first 12 sts, K 16; work in pattern across next 60 sts, K 16; work in pattern across last 12 sts.

Row 54: YO, purl across.

Row 55: Repeat Row 53.

Row 56: Purl.

Rows 57-76: Rep Rows 53-56, five more times.

Row 77: Work in pattern across first 12 sts, K 16; work in pattern across next 16 sts, K 28; work in pattern across next 16 sts, K 16; work in pattern across last 12 sts.

Row 78: YO, purl across.

Row 79: Repeat Row 77.

Row 80: Purl .

Rows 81-124: Rep Rows 77-80, eleven more times.

Rows 125-148: Rep Rows 53-76.

Rows 149-164: Rep Rows 37-52.

Rows 165-200: Rep Rows 1-36. Bind off loosely.

Multi-Color Striped

*F*or lovers of single crochet, making this afghan will be a true delight. Try your own color combinations: soft pastels or bright shades will completely change the look. In our colors, its a nice gift for just about anyone

Size

49" x 56" before fringing

Materials

Worsted weight yarn:
20 oz navy
12 oz country blue
4 oz lt country blue
8 oz heather
8 oz medium country blue

(Photographed model made in Bernat® Berella® "4"® Colors #08965, Navy (A); #01108 True Country Blue (B); #08720 Lt Country Blue (C); #01010, Soft Heather (D); #08721, Med Country Blue (E))

Size I (5.5 mm) crochet hook (or size required for gauge)

Gauge

10 sts = 2 $\frac{1}{2}$"

continued on the next page

Multi-Color Striped

Notes

Notes

1. In starting and ending each new color sequence, leave an 8" yarn end. These will be used later as part of the fringe.

2. When changing colors, pull new color through last 2 loops to complete sc.

Instructions

Using Color A, chain 200; afghan is worked lengthwise.

Row 1 (right side): Sc in 2nd ch from hook; * ch 1, skip 1 ch, sc in next ch; rep from * across, ch 1, turn.

Row 2: Sc in first sc; * ch 1, skip ch-1 space, sc in next sc; rep from * across, ch 1, turn.

Repeat Row 2 only for pattern, always working ch-1 over a ch-1 space and sc over sc.

Work in stripe pattern as follows:

2 rows each of A, B, E, B, C

4 rows of A

1 row of D

Repeat these 15 rows 9 times, ending by working Row 15. Always start the first of these 15 rows on right side of work.

Fringe

Follow Single Knot Fringe Instructions on page 140. Cut yarn strands 16" in length in all colors. Working across the long end of afghan where partial fringe has already been made, using 1 strand, make a knot at every color change twice where there is no fringe; and once at the area where there is already a self-made fringe.

Marvelous Mauve Lapghan

Here's a pretty way to keep your knees warm, done in shades of mauve. This is an unusual design, with a motif inserted in each outer corner.

Marvelous Mauve Lapghan

Size

36" x 46"

Materials

Worsted weight yarn:

14 oz heather

5 oz lt mauve

9 oz mauve

(Photographed model made in Bernat®
Berella® "4"® Colors #01010 Soft
Heather; #01305, Soft Mauve;
#01306 True Mauve)

Size H (8 mm) crochet hook (or size
required for gauge)

Gauge

One square motif = 7" x 7"

Instructions

Square (make 10)

With lt mauve, ch 4, join with a sl st to
form a ring.

Rnd 1: Ch 3 (counts as 1 dc), 2 dc in ring;
* ch 1, 3 dc in ring; rep from * 2 times,
ch 1; join with sl st to top ch of beg ch-3;
finish off.

Rnd 2: Join mauve in any ch 1 sp, ch 3
(counts as 1 dc), in same sp work (2 dc, ch
2, 3 dc): beg corner made; ch 1; * in next
ch 1 sp, work (3 dc, ch 2, 3 dc): corner
made; ch 1; rep from * 2 more times; join
with sl st in top ch of beg ch-3; finish off.

Rnd 3: Join heather in any ch 2 sp,(ch 3, 2
dc, ch 2, 3 dc) in same sp; * ch 1, 3 dc in
next ch-1 sp, ch 1; (3dc, ch 2, 3dc) in next
ch-2 corner sp; rep from * twice more; ch
1, 3 dc in next ch 1 sp, ch 1, join to top ch
of beg ch-3. Do not fasten off, sl st across
to next corner ch-2 sp.

Rnds 4 through 6: Rep Rnd 3, working
one additional (ch 1, 3-dc) group along
each side as required. Finish off, weave
in ends.

Joining

Hold two motifs with right sides facing; carefully matching sts, sew or sc motifs together. Repeat twice. Join pairs of motifs in rows of two across and 3 down.

Edging

Rnd 1: Join lt mauve with a sl st in any outer ch-2 corner space; in same sp work (2 dc, ch 2, 3 dc); * in each ch-1 sp work (ch 1, 3 dc, ch 1); in each ch-2 sp work (3 dc, ch 2, 3 dc); rep from * around, ending (ch 1, 3 dc, ch 1) in each ch-1 sp, join.

Rnd 2: Sl st into next ch-2 sp; continue as for Rnd 1, finish off.

Rnds 3 through 7: Continuing in same pattern, work three rows of mauve and four rows of heather. Finish off.

Outside Border (work in rows on one edge only)

Row 1: Join mauve in any heather corner ch-2 sp, ch 3, 2 dc in same sp; * ch 1, 3 dc in next ch 1 sp, ch 1; rep from * to next corner ch-2 sp, 3 dc in corner sp, ch 4, turn.

Row 2: 3 dc in first ch-1 sp; * ch 1, 3 dc in next ch-1 sp; rep from * across and into last ch 1 sp; ch 1, dc in top of ch-3; ch 3, turn.

Row 3: 2 dc in ch-1 sp; * ch 1, 3 dc in next ch-1 sp; rep from * across, , ending with ch 1, 1 dc into top of ch-3 of previous row. Finish off.

Rows 4 and 5: With lt mauve, rep rows 1 and 2. Finish off.

Rows 6 through 11: With heather, rep rows 1 and 2. Finish off.

Work remaining 3 sides in the same way. Then sew a motif into each corner.

Final Border

Note:

Work around entire afghan, working across each outside border section and around the outer two sides of each corner motif.

Row 1: Join lt mauve to any corner motif at corner ch-2 sp. Ch 3, (2 dc, ch 2, 3 dc) in same sp, * work (ch 1, 3 dc in next ch-1 sp) along edge of afghan to ch-2 sp at next afghan corner, ch 1, (3 dc, ch 2, 3 dc) in corner sp; rep from * twicw more, work ch 1, 3 dc in next ch-1 sp along last edge to beg corner, ch 1; join to top of ch-3.

Row 2: With lt mauve, sl st to corner ch-2 sp, then work as for Row 1. Finish off lt mauve.

Row 3: With mauve, rep Row 1.

Row 4: With mauve, rep Row 2.

Weave in all loose ends.

Blue Lagoon

The blues and greens of a serene lagoon inspired this restful afghan. You'll love wrapping it around you for a serene nap. The open pattern is easy and fast to crochet

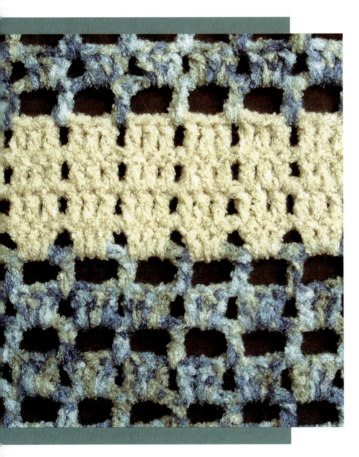

Size

45" x 60" before fringing

Materials

Worsted weight yarn:
20 oz ombre
8 oz green

(Photographed afghan was made with TLC® Amoré™ #3995 Lagoon Print and #3625 Celery)

Size H (5 mm) crochet hook (or size required for gauge)

Gauge

(3 dc + one ch-1 sp) = 1"
4 rows dc = 2$^{1}/_{2}$"

Note

To change colors, YO, draw up a lp in last st (3 lps on hook), YO, draw through 2 lps; change to new color, YO, draw through rem 2 lps.

continued on the next page

Blue Lagoon

Instructions

With ombre yarn, ch 181 loosely.

Row 1: Dc in 4th ch from hook and in next ch, ch 1; * dc in next 3 chs, ch 1, sk next ch; rep from * across to last 3 chs, dc in last 3 chs: 135 dc, counting beg skipped chs as a dc, and 44 ch-1 sps, ch 6, turn.

Row 2: Dc in first ch-1 sp; * ch 3, dc in next ch-1 sp; rep from * across, ending ch 3, dc in top of turning ch; ch 3, turn.

Row 3: 2 dc in first ch-3 sp; * ch 1, 3 dc in next ch-3 sp; rep from * across, work last dc in 3rd ch of turning ch-6, turn.

Rep Rows 2 and 3, five times; then repeat Row 2 once, joining green in last st. You should have 14 rows of ombre; ch 3, turn.

Row 15: With green, rep Row 3, but at end, ch 3 instead of 6, turn.

Row 16: Dc in next 2 dc; * ch 1, dc in next 3 dc; rep from * across, ch 3, turn.

Rows 17 and 18: Rep Row 16. At last st on Row 18, join ombre yarn, finish off green.

Rows 19 through 31: Rep Rows 2 and 3 six times, then Row 2 once more.

Rows 32 through 35: Rep Rows 15 through 18.

Now rep Rows 19 through 35, three times; with ombre, rep Rows 2 and 3, seven times. Finish off, weave in all loose ends.

Border

Row 1: Working on one long edge of afghan, join green at corner, ch 1, 2 sc in side of dc; * 2 sc in ch-3 sp, sc around dc; rep from * across ombre rows; on solid rows, ** sc around dc, ch 1, rep from ** across solid rows; continue in this manner across edge to top corner, ending by working 2 sc in last ch-3 sp; ch 1, turn.

Row 2: Sc in each sc and ch-1 sp across row, finish off. Work same border on other long edge.

Fringe

Follow Single Knot Fringe Instructions on page 140. Cut 180 strands, 16" long using green. Use 4 strands, folded in half, for each knot and tie knot at the ch-1 space across each short end of afghan (44 knots each side).

Peppermint Candy Baby Afghan

Here's a fun concept in crochet — a pinwheel circle afghan! What a great shower gift this would make. It's fun and fast to crochet on a big size K hook. If you prefer, make it in pink and white for a girl or blue and white for a boy.

Peppermint Candy Baby Afghan

Size

45" diameter

Materials

Worsted weight yarn:
12 oz red
12 oz white

(Photographed model made with TLC®
Essentials™ Colors #2913 Ranch Red
and #2101 White.)

Size K (6.5 mm) crochet hook (or size
required for gauge)

Gauge

2 sc and 2 ch-1 sps = 1"
3 rows = 1"

Instructions

Starting at center with white, loosely ch 71.

Row 1: Sc in 3rd ch from hook; * ch 1, sk 1
ch, sc in next ch; rep from * across row: 35
sc and 34 ch-1 sps; ch 2, turn.

Row 2: Sk first sc, sc in next sp; * ch 1, sc
in next sp; rep from * to last sc, ch 1, sc in
sp under turning ch; ch 2, turn.

Row 3 (short row): Sc in first sp; * ch 1, sc in next sp; rep from * to last 3 sc, ch 1, sl st in next sp, leave last sp unworked; ch 1, turn.

Row 4: Sk first sl st and next sc, sc in next sp; * ch 1, sc in next sp; rep from * to last sc, ch 1, sc in sp under turning ch; ch 2, turn.

Row 5 (short row): Sc in first sp; * ch 1, sc in next sp; rep from * to last 2 sc of prev row, ch 1, sl st in next sp; ch 1, turn.

Rows 6 through 33: Rep Rows 4 and 5, 14 times more.

Row 34: Sk first sl st and next sc, sc in next sp, ch 1, sc in sp under turning ch; end at outer edge and draw red through 2 lps of last sc, cut white; with red, ch 2, turn.

**** Long Row:** * Sc in first sp; * ch 1, sc in sp between next sc and sl st, ch 1, sc in next sp (where sl st was worked); rep from * to last 2 sc, ch 1, sc in next sp, ch 1, sc in sp under turning ch: 35 sc and 34 ch-1 sps; ch 1, turn.

Rep Rows 2 through 34; end at outer edge and draw white through 2 lps of last sc, cut old color; ch 2, turn. **

Repeat from ** to **, alternating colors.

At end of last row, do not cut yarn; you should have 12 color sections in all.

Joining

Continuing with red, crochet first and last sections together as follows: Hold sections with right sides together and carefully matching sps along one edge with ch-1 sps along other edge, work instructions for Long Row, ending at center.

Finish off, leaving 10" end. Thread into tapestry or yarn needle and weave through sts around center opening, draw up tightly and fasten securely.

Border

Rnd 1: With right side facing you, join white in any outer edge st, work (sc, ch 1) evenly spaced around, join with a sl st in beg sc; cut white, with red ch 1, do not turn.

Rnd 2: With red, sc in next sp; * ch 1, sc in next sp; rep from * around, ch 1, join with a sl st in beg sc; cut red, with white, ch 1, do not turn.

Rep Rnd 2 once more with white.

At end of last rnd, finish off and weave in all loose ends. Lightly steam.

*E*asy and quick, this lovely throw has a light lacey look, accented with cables.

Vanilla Lace Throw

Size
36" x 46"

Materials
Worsted weight yarn:
18 oz cream

(Photographed model made with TLC® Amoré™ Color #3103 Vanilla)

Size 10 (6 mm) circular needle (or size required for gauge)

Gauge
12 sts = 3"

Instructions
Cast on 144 sts loosely.

Row 1: Knit.

Row 2: Purl.

Row 3: K 1; * YO twice, K 1; rep from * across.

Row 4: * Sl 6 sts as to purl, dropping YO sts; this will form 6 long loops on right needle. With left needle, pick up the first group of 3 sts and pass first group over the second group of 3 sts. Now all 6 sts are on left needle; purl each of these 6 sts; rep from * across.

Row 5: Knit.

Row 6: Purl.

Rep these 6 rows until 32 pattern rows have been completed. Bind off loosely, weave in all yarn ends.

Fringe
Following Single Knot Fringe instructions on page 140 cut strands into 14" lengths; double strands and knot one strand into each st across short ends.

*R*ows of cross stitches add texture interest to this feminine afghan designed to warm your knees on a cold morning.

In the Pink

Size
36" x 36"

Materials
Worsted weight yarn:
18 oz pink

(Photographed model made in Caron® Simply Soft®, Color #9719 Soft Pink)

Size J (6 mm) crochet hook (or size required for gauge)

Gauge
3 dc = 1"

Instructions
Ch 110 loosely; afghan is worked lengthwise.

Row 1: Dc in 4th chain from hook and in each ch across: 108 dc, counting beg skipped chs as a st; ch 3 (counts as first dc of following row throughout), turn.

Row 2: Dc in each dc across, dc in top of ch-3; ch 3, turn.

Row 3: Rep Row 2.

Row 4: * Skip next dc, dc in next dc, dc in skipped dc (cross stitch made dc); rep from * across, ending dc in top of ch-3; ch 3, turn.

Rows 5-7: Rep Row 4.

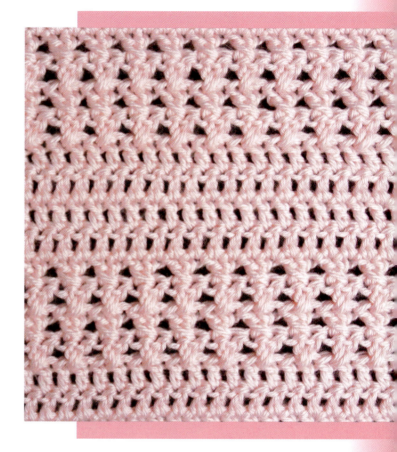

Rows 8 and 9: Rep Row 2.

Repeat rows 2 through 9 until piece measures about 36", rep Row 2 once more. Finish off, weave in all ends.

Fringe
Follow Single Knot Fringe Instructions on page 140. Cut strands 16" long, and use 2 strands folded for each knot. Tie knots around the ch-3 or dc post across each short end of afghan.

This beautiful, traditional pattern stitch originated in the Scottish Shetland Islands, where the famous Shetland lace knit shawls were created. This was one of the most popular of the lace stitches. Our afghan works up quickly on size 11 needles, and is made in three panels. We made our model in an ombre yarn, but it would be just as pretty worked in a solid color.

Easy Feather and Fan

Size
44" x 60"

Materials
Worsted weight yarn:
30 oz ombre

(Photographed model made with Caron® Rainbow Dreams Color #599 Rosy Forecast)

Size 11 (8 mm) knitting needles (or size required for gauge)

Gauge
In garter stitch (knit every row):
14 sts = 4"

Instructions
Panel (make 3)
Cast on 54 sts.

Bottom Border: Knit six rows.

Pattern Rows
Row 1 (right side): Knit.

Row 2: Purl.

Row 3: * (K 2 tog) 3 times; (YO, K 1) 6 times; (K 2 tog) 3 times; rep from * across row.

Row 4: Knit.

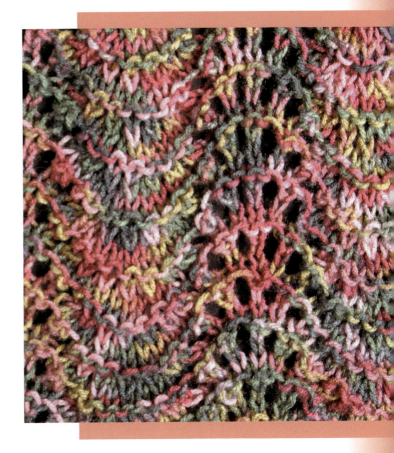

Rep Rows 1 through 4 until piece measures about 59" long, ending by working Row 2 of Pattern Rows.

Top Border: Knit six rows. Bind off loosely.

Finishing
With right sides facing, join two panels along edge with overcast stitch, taking care to match rows carefully. Do not pull yarn too tightly as you sew. Join third panel in same manner.

Blue Rhapsody

*W*onderfully soft bulky yarn works up quickly and makes a warm afghan. The blue and white colors create a nice contrast.

Size

43" x 54"

Materials

Bulky weight yarn:
12 oz blue (Color A)
18 oz white (Color B)

(Photographed model was made with Lion Brand Jiffy®, Colors #109 Royal (A) and #100 White (B)

36" size 11 (8 mm) circular needle (or size required for gauge)

Gauge

12 sts = 4"

Note

Circular needle is used to accommodate large number of stitches; do not join, work back and forth in rows.

continued on the next page

Blue Rhapsody

Pattern Stitch

Row 1 (right side): K 1; * with yarn in back, sl 1 as to purl, K 1; rep from * across, ending K 1.

Row 2: K 1; * with yarn in front, sl 1 as to purl, K 1; rep from * across, ending K 1.

Rows 3 and 4: Knit.

These four rows comprise one pattern.

Instructions

With Color B, cast on 129 sts.

Work 5 patterns of Color B (20 rows)

3 patterns of Color A (12 rows)

4 patterns of Color B (16 rows)

3 patterns of Color A (12 rows)

Repeat above sequence two more times, then work 5 patterns (20 rows) of Color B.

Bind off loosely.

Fringe

Follow Single Knot Fringe Instructions on page 140. Using Color B, cut strands 16" long, and use 2 strands folded in half for each knot. Tie knot through every other stitch across each short end.

Pink Petals

This pretty pink confection is crocheted in an attractive V-Stitch, combined with double crochet.

Pink Petals

Size
39" x 40"

Materials
Worsted weight yarn:
15 oz pink

(Photographed model made with Lion Brand Imagine, Color #101)

Size J (6 mm) crochet hook (or size required for gauge)

Gauge
8 dc = 3"

Instructions
Chain 105 loosely; afghan is worked lengthwise.

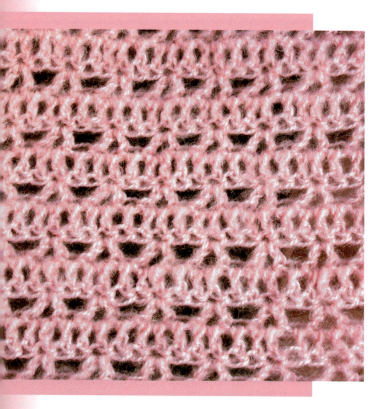

Foundation Row 1: Dc in 4th ch from hook and in each ch across: 103 dc; ch 2, turn (counts as 1 dc).

Row 2: Skip first dc, dc in next dc and in each dc across, ending by making a dc in top of beg ch-3; ch 2, turn.

Pattern
Row 1: Skip next dc, dc in next dc; sk 1 dc (dc, ch 1, dc) all in next dc (V-St made); * skip 2 dc, (dc, ch 1, dc) all in next dc; rep from * across, to last 3 sts, skip next dc, dc in next dc, dc under the ch-2: 33 V-sts with 2 dc at each end; ch 2, turn.

Row 2: Skip first dc; dc in each dc, ch 1 and dc of each V-St: 103 sts; ch 2, turn.

Row 3: Skip first dc, dc in next st, skip next st, V-St in next st; * skip 2 sts, V-St in next st; rep from * across, end skip next dc, dc in next dc, dc under the ch-2: 33 V-Sts with 2 dc at each end; ch 2, turn.

Rep Pattern rows 2 and 3 until afghan measures 37", ending by working Row 2 of pattern. Rep Row 2 once more. Finish off. Weave in all loose ends.

Border
Work a Shell Stitch pattern along each short end of afghan. With right side of work facing, attach yarn under corner dc bar; ch 1, work shell of (sc, hdc, dc, hdc, sc) in same space; * work another shell around the ch-2 of the V-St row; rep from * across edge, ending with a shell around the ch-2 of the dc row; fasten off.

Stripes on Parade

Two yarn colors are combined in this afghan for a striking three-color effect. The yarn is worked with two strands throughout, sometimes two of blue, sometimes two of white, sometimes one strand of each color. The stitch is an easy, fun to work cross stitch.

Stripes on Parade

Size

29" x 40" before fringing

Materials

Worsted weight yarn:
22 oz white
26 oz blue

(Photographed model made with TLC®
Essentials™, Colors #2101 White and
#2816 Powder Blue)

Size L (8 mm) crochet hook (or size
required for gauge)

Gauge

In pattern, 11 sts = 4$\frac{1}{2}$"

Note

To change colors, draw up a lp in last st
(2 lps on hook), change to new color,
YO, draw through both lps. Cut off old
color.

Instructions

Using 2 strands of blue, ch 97 loosely; afghan is worked lengthwise.

Row 1: Sc in 2nd ch from hook and in each rem ch: 96 sc; turn.

Row 2: Ch 3 (counts as first dc of row); * skip next sc, dc in each of next 2 sc, dc in skipped sc (cross stitch made); rep from * across ending dc in last sc: 31 cross stitches; ch 1, turn.

Row 3: Sc in each dc, sc in top of turning ch; ch 3, turn.

Rows 4 through 9: Repeat Rows 2 and 3, 3 more times. Change ONE of the strands of Blue to White on last st of Row 9.

Rows 10 through 15: Using one strand of blue and one of white, rep Rows 2 and 3, 3 times, changing the one strand of blue to white on the last stitch of Row 15.

Rows 16 through 19: Using 2 strands of white, rep Rows 2 and 3, twice; changing to 2 strands of blue on last st of Row 19.

Rows 20-23: Using 2 strands of blue, rep Rows 2 and 3, twice, changing to 2 strands of white on last st of row 23.

Rows 24-27: Rep Rows 16-19 (2 strands white).

Rows 28-31: Rep Rows 20-23 (2 strands blue).

Rows 32-35: Rep Rows 16-19 (2 strands white).

Rows 36-41: Rep Rows 10-15(1 strand of each color).

Rows 42-49: Rep Rows 2-9 (2 strands blue); at end of Row 49, finish off, weave in all loose ends.

Fringe

Follow Single Knot Fringe Instructions on page 140. Cut strands of each color 16" long. Working across each short end, use 6 folded strands of blue, and tie a knot around the ch-3 post of Row 2. Rep across, matching solid color knots and mixed color knots to afghan.

Lovely Lace

*S*tripes of celery and cream dress up this easy to knit afghan featuring a mock cable pattern.

Size

35" x 38"

Materials

Worsted weight yarn:

6 oz cream (A)

6 oz celery (B)

(Photographed model made with TLC® Amoré™, Colors #3101 Vanilla (A); and #3625 Celery (B))

29" size 10½ (6.5 mm) circular needle (or size required for gauge)

2 stitch markers

Gauge

In Garter Stitch (knit every row):

12 sts = 3"

Note

There is an 8-stitch Garter St border on each side of afghan; markers are used after the first eight Garter Sts and before the last eight Garter Sts for ease in working pattern; slip markers on each row.

continued on the next page

Lovely Lace

Instructions
Bottom Border
With Color A, cast on 116 sts loosely. Knit 12 rows. Cut Color A, join Color B.

Row 1 (wrong side): K 8, place marker on needle; K 1; * P 2, K 2; rep from * across, to last 11 sts, P 2, K 1; place marker on needle, K 8.

Row 2: K 8, P 1; * K 1, YO, K 1; P 2; rep from * to last 11 sts, K 1, YO, K 1, P 1; K 8.

Row 3: K 8; K 1, * P 3, K 2; rep from * to last 12 sts, P 3, K 1; K 8.

Row 4: K 8; P 1, * K 3, pass first K st over the next 2 K sts; P 2; rep from * to last 12 sts, K 3, pass first K st over next 2 K sts, P 1; K 8.

Rep Rows 1–4, 3 times more (except on Row 1, sl markers rather than place them). Finish off Color B, join Color A.

Repeating Rows 1 through 4 for pattern, work in following color sequence:

4 rows Color A

4 rows Color B

4 rows Color A

4 rows Color B

16 rows Color A

4 rows Color B

4 rows Color A

4 rows Color B

4 rows Color A

16 rows Color B

4 rows Color A

4 rows Color B

4 rows Color A

4 rows Color B

16 rows Color A

4 rows Color B

4 rows Color A

4 rows Color B

Top Border
With Color A, knit 12 rows. Bind off loosely; weave in loose ends.

Raspberries and Cream

Raspberry pink and creamy white yarns are combined for a fresh, springtime look that's good enough to eat! The easy 4-row pattern uses slipped stitches to create a checkered effect.

Raspberries and Cream

Size

32" x 36"

Materials

Worsted weight yarn:
9 oz pink (Color A)
6 oz white (Color B)

(Photographed model made in TLC® Essentials™ Colors #2772 Lt. Country Rose (A) and #2101 White (B))

2 stitch markers

14" size 10½ (6.5 mm) straight needles (or size required for gauge)

Gauge

7 sts = 2"
9 rows = 2"

Notes

1. Afghan has a 7-st Seed Stitch border on each side. Seed Stitch is worked on an uneven number of stitches as follows:

* K 1, P 1, rep from * across row, ending K 1.

Markers are placed on Row 1 after the 7th st and before the last 7 sts for ease in following pattern. Slip markers on all following rows.

2. Pattern is worked alternately in two rows of each color; do not cut yarn not in use; carry loosely up side of work.

Instructions

With Color A, cast on 113 sts loosely.

Bottom Border

Row 1: * K 1, P 1; rep from * across row ending K 1.

Repeat this row until border measures 2"; do not cut A.

Pattern Rows

Row 1: With Color B, (K 1, P 1) 3 times, K 1, place a marker on right needle to indicate end of Seed St side border; K 2, * with yarn in back of work, sl 1 as to purl, K 2; rep from * to last 9 sts, K 2; place a marker on right needle to indicate beginning of Seed St side border; work in Seed St across last 7 sts.

Row 2: Seed over 7 sts; P 2, * with yarn in front, slip 1 st as to purl, P 2; rep from * to marker, Seed over last 7 sts. Drop Color B.

Row 3: With Color A, Seed over 7 sts; knit to last 7 sts, Seed over last 7 sts.

Row 4: Seed over 7 sts; purl to last 7 sts, Seed over last 7 sts.

Rep Rows 1 through 4 until piece measures about 34" from cast-on row, ending by working Row 2; cut off Color B.

Top Border

With Color A, rep Bottom Border Row 1 for 2"; bind off loosely in Seed St. Weave in all loose ends.

Delightful Daisies

The pretty flower-like stitch of this afghan combines with lovely, soft yarn to create a beautiful afghan for the new baby. Try it in other soft pastels, too, or in bright white.

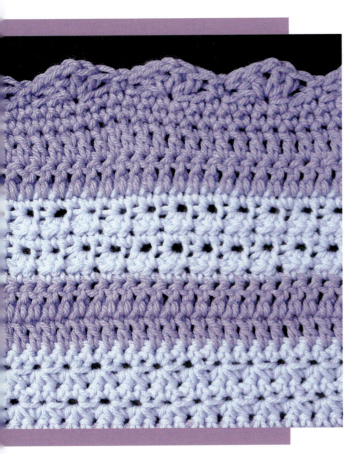

Size

26" x 37"

Materials

Worsted weight yarn:
20 oz lilac
10 oz blue

(Photographed model made with Bernat® Berella® "4"®, Colors #01317 Lilac and #08944 Baby Blue)

Size K (6.5 mm) crochet hook (or size required for gauge)

Size I (5.5 mm) crochet hook

Gauge

With K hook, 3 dc = 1"
2 Daisy rows = 1^1/$_2$"

Note

To change color at end of row, work across, YO, draw up a lp in last st (3 lps on hook), YO, draw through 2 lps, change to new color; YO, draw through rem 2 lps, ch 3, turn.

continued on the next page

Delightful Daisies

Instructions

With lilac and K hook, ch 84 sts loosely.

Row 1: Dc in 4th ch from hook and in each ch across: 82 dc, counting beg skipped ch as a dc; ch 2, turn.

Row 2: Dc in each dc and in top of turning ch, joining blue on last st; ch 1, turn. Finish off Color A.

Row 3: Sc in each dc across, ch 2, (counts as a dc on following rows) turn.

Row 4 (Daisy Row): Insert hook in 2nd ch from hook, YO, draw a lp through (2 lps on hook), insert hook in first sc, YO, draw a lp through; draw a lp through each of the next 2 sc, YO, draw lp through all 5 lps on hook, ch 1 (Daisy made); * insert hook in center lp of Daisy just made, YO, draw a lp through; insert hook in last ch-1 of Daisy just made and pull lp through; draw a lp through each of next 2 sc, YO, draw a lp through all 5 lps, ch 1; rep from * for pattern, ending by working a dc under turning ch: 40 Daisy patterns. Ch 1, turn.

Row 5: Skip first stitch, sc in next st and in each st across, ch 2, turn.

Row 6: Repeat Row 4.

Row 7: Repeat Row 5, changing to lilac in last stitch; fasten off blue, leaving a 4" yarn end for weaving later; ch 2, turn.

Row 8: With lilac, sk first sc, dc in next sc and in each st across; ch 2, turn.

Rep Rows 2 through 8 for pattern, until afghan measures about 36", ending by working Row 2.

Border

Using size I hook:

Rnd 1: On right side with top row of afghan facing, attach lilac to corner of last dc row. Work sc in each dc across to corner, work 3 sc in corner. Work sc in each dc bar to next dc corner (adjust sc sts to keep work flat). Work 3 sc in corner and in each dc to next corner; work 3 sc in corner and sc evenly spaced along side to beginning corner; slip stitch into sc at beg of round.

Rnd 2: Ch 1, sc in first sc and in each sc around, working 3 sc in each corner sc. Slip stitch in top of beg of rnd.

Rnd 3: Slip stitch to middle sc of next corner; sc, skip 2 sc; * (2 dc, ch 1, 2 dc: shell made) in next st; skip 2 sts, sc in next sc. Rep from * to next corner, ending with a shell, sc in top of 3 sc group in corner. Finish off. Weave in all loose ends.

Pretty Stripes

This is a beautiful and easy to crochet design, perfect for the beginner. The pattern can be adapted to any color scheme; try it in shades of blue with lilac; beiges and oranges; or use six bright and bold different shades for a striking effect. Because it's worked with two strands of yarn held together, you'll have an afghan in no time!

Pretty Stripes

Size
42" x 60"

Materials
Worsted weight yarn:

8 oz lt rose

8 oz med rose

8 oz dk rose

8 oz lt mauve

8 oz med mauve

8 oz dk burgundy

6 oz natural

(Photographed model made with Bernat® Berella® "4"® Colors #08940, Natural; #08814 Pale Antique Rose; #08815 Lt Antique Rose; #08816 Medium Antique Rose; #01305 Soft Mauve; #01306 True Mauve; #01405, Dark Burgundy)

Size K (6.5 mm) crochet hook (or size required for gauge)

Gauge
With two strands of yarn held togeher,

5 tr = 2"

2 rows = 2 1/2 "

Instructions

Strip (make 1 strip in every color except natural)

With two yarn strands held together, ch 110.

Row 1 (right side): Tr in 5th ch from hook and in each ch across: 107 tr, counting skipped ch-4 as a tr; ch 4, turn.

Rows 2-9: Skip first tr, tr in back loop only of each tr across, tr in top of turning ch; ch 4, turn. At end of last row, omit ch 4, finish off. Weave in ends.

Joining

Hold Row 9 of lt rose and starting ch of med rose strips together, with wrong sides facing. With two strands of natural, working through both strips, sc in each st across long edge; finish off. In same manner, join remaining strips in this order: dk rose, lt, med and dk mauve.

Fringe

Following instructions for Single Knot Fringe on page 140 cut natural strands 18" long. Use 4 strands, folded in half, for each knot. Knot fringe in every other stitch across each narrow end.

Rosy Future

*P*opcorn stitches give a raised dimension to these bright squares. The afghan will bring both warmth and beauty to a cold wintery day.

Size
50" x 68"

Materials
Worsted weight yarn:
28 oz garnet (dk rose)
12 oz rose
12 oz green

(Photographed model made with TLC® Amoré™, Colors #3782 Garnet, #3710 Rose, and #3623 Celery)

Size I (5.5 mm) crochet hook (or size required for gauge)

Gauge
One square = 9"

Instructions
Square Motif (make 35)
With rose, ch 6, join with a sl st to form a ring.

Rnd 1: Work beg PC (popcorn) in ring as follows: Ch 3, work 3 dc in ring; drop lp from hook; insert hook in top of beg ch-3; hook dropped lp and pull through st: beg PC made; * ch 3, work PC in ring as follows: Work 4 dc in ring; drop lp from hook, insert hook in first dc of 4-dc group just made; hook dropped lp and pull through st: PC made. Rep from * twice more; ch 3, join with a sl st in top of ch-3 of beg PC.

continued on the next page

Rosy Future

Rnd 2: Sl st into next ch-3 sp; work (beg PC; ch 3, PC) in same sp; * ch 3, (PC, ch 3, PC) in next ch-3 sp; rep from * twice more. ch 3; join with a sl st in top of ch-3 of beg PC. Finish off rose.

Note

Be sure to leave 4" end when finishing off or joining a color to weave in later.

Rnd 3: Join green with a sl st in any ch-3 sp between 2 corners (corner is 2 PCs worked in SAME sp). Ch 3, 2 dc in same sp; (3 dc, ch 3, 3 dc) in next ch-3 sp for corner; * 3 dc in next ch-3 sp between corners; (3 dc, ch 3, 3 dc) in next ch-3 sp for corner; rep from * twice more; join with a sl st in top of beg ch-3.

Rnd 4: Sl st in each of next 2 dc, then sl st into sp between pair of 3-dc groups, ch 3, 2 dc in same sp; (3 dc, ch 3, 3 dc) in next ch-3 sp at corner; * 3 dc between each pair of 3-dc groups along side, (3 dc, ch 3, 3 dc) in next ch-3 sp at corner; rep from * twice more; work 3 dc between last pair of 3-dc groups, join with a sl st in top of beg ch-3. Finish off green.

Rnd 5: Join dk rose with a sl st in any corner ch-3 sp; ch 3, (2 dc, ch 3, 3 dc) in same sp; * 3 dc between each pair of 3-dc groups along side, (3 dc, ch 3, 3 dc) in next ch-3 sp at corner; rep from * twice more; 3 dc between each pair of 3-dc groups along last side, join with a sl st in top of beg ch-3.

Rnd 6: Sl l st in each of next 2 dc, then sl st into ch-3 corner sp; now work rnd in same manner as Rnd 5.

Rnd 7: Rep Rnd 6; finish off dark rose.

Rnd 8: With Green, rep Rnd 5. Finish off, weave in all ends.

Finishing

Afghan is 5 squares wide by 7 squares long. Join squares tog, with right sides facing, and with green yarn, work sc through back lp only of each stitch.

Border

With right side facing you, join green with a sl st in any ch-3 corner sp of afghan. Working in same manner as Rnd 5 of Square, work one rnd in each of the following colors: green, rose, green and dk rose When all 4 rnds of border have been completed, finish off and weave in all loose yarn ends.

Roses in the Snow

Bright red roses burst through the snow to brighten the gray days of winter. The octagon motifs make an interesting geometric pattern.

Roses in the Snow

Size
50" x 72"

Materials
Worsted weight yarn:
10 oz red
8 oz black
8 oz gray
10 oz white

(Photographed model was made with Red Heart® Classic Colors #902 Jockey Red, #12 Black, #401 Nickel (gray), and #1 White)

Size H (5 mm) crochet hook, or size required for gauge

Gauge
4 dc = 1"
One motif measures 8" from point to opposite point.

Instructions
Hexagon Motif (make 59)
With red, ch 5, join to form a ring.

Rnd 1: Ch 4 (counts as a tr throughout), 17 tr in ring, join to top of beg ch-4: 18 tr.

Rnd 2: Ch 4 , 6 tr in same st as joining ; * sk 2 sts, 7 tr in next st; rep from * around, join as before: six 7-tr groups. Finish off red.

Rnd 3: Join white in space between any two 7-dc groups; ch 4, 6 tr in same sp; * 3 dc in 4th tr of next 7-tr group, 7 tr in space between next this and next 7-tr group; rep from * around, ending 3 dc in 4th tr of last 7-tr group; join, finish off white.

Rnd 4: Join gray in center tr of any 7-tr group, ch 3, 2 dc in same st; * dc in each st to center tr of next 7 tr group, 3 dc in center tr; rep from * around, ending dc in each st of last side, join. Finish off gray.

Rnd 5: Join black in center dc of any 3-dc group; ch 1, 3 sc in same st; * sc in each st to center st of next 3-dc group, 3 dc in center dc; rep from * around, ending sc in each st of last side, join. Finish off black.

Weave in all yarn ends.

Finishing

With black and right sides facing, join motifs following Assembly Diagram.

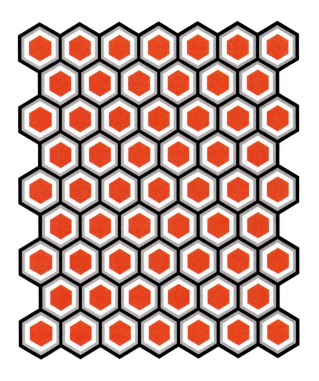

Edging

With black, work sc all around outer edge of afghan, working 3 sc in each corner sp; finish off.

This is a classic favorite pattern that has been handed down from generation to generation. Knitted on large needles, it has a lovely, lacey look.

Feather and Fan

Size
46" x 50"

Materials
Worsted weight yarn:
18 oz blue variegated

(Photographed model made with Lion Brand Imagine Color #328 Moody Blues)

36" size 10 (6 mm) circular needle (or size required for gauge)

Gauge
Each fan point = 4$\frac{1}{2}$"

Instructions
Loosely cast on 192 sts; do not join; work back and forth in rows.

Row 1: Knit.

Row 2: (K 2 tog) 4 times; (YO, K 1) 8 times; * (K 2 tog) 8 times; (YO, K 1) 8 times; rep from* 6 more times; (K 2 tog) 4 times.

Row 3: Knit.

Row 4: Purl.

Rep these four rows for pattern; work until piece measures about 50", ending by working Row 4. Bind off loosely.

Ocean Waves

The lovely colors and wave-like pattern of this afghan remind us of the ocean. And you'll have oceans of fun making it quickly in double crochet on a J hook.

Size

50" x 60"

Materials

Worsted weight yarn:

24 oz navy (Color A)

12 oz lt blue (Color B)

8 oz med blue (Color C)

(Photographed model made with TLC® Essentials™ Colors #2855 Navy (A), #2816 Powder Blue (B), and #2883 Country Blue (C))

Size J (6 mm) crochet hook (or size required for gauge)

Gauge

7 sts = 2"

4 rows = 2$\frac{1}{2}$"

Instructions

With Color A, ch 170.

Row 1: Draw up a lp in 2nd and 3rd chs from hook, YO and draw through all 3 lps on hook: sc decrease made; * sc in next 10 chs, 3 sc in next ch, sc in next 10 chs; draw up a lp in each of next 3 chs, YO and draw through all 4 lps on hook; rep from * 5 more times; sc in next 10 chs, 3 sc in next ch, sc in next 10 chs; draw up a lp in each of last 2 chs and complete a sc: 169 sts; ch 3, turn.

continued on the next page

Ocean Waves

Row 2: Skip first st, dc in next 11 sts; * 3 dc in next st, dc in next 10 sts; holding back last lp of each dc, dc in next 3 sts, YO and draw through all lps on hook; dc in next 10 sts; repeat from * 5 more times; 3 dc in next st, dc in next 10 sts; holding back last lp of each dc, dc in each of last 2 sts, YO and draw through all lps on hook; ch 3, turn.

Row 3: Working in back lp only of each st, work as for Row 2 to within last 2 dc (do not count ch-3 as a dc), dec 1 dc over last 2 sts, do not work in top of ch-3; ch 3, turn.

Row 4: Working through both lps of each dc, work as for Row 2 to within last 2 dc, dec 1 dc over last 2 dc (do not work in top of ch-3); ch 3, turn.

Repeating Rows 3 and 4 for pattern, work in pattern in the following color sequence:

* 2 rows Color A

2 rows Color C

4 rows Color A

2 rows Color C

6 rows Color A

6 rows Color B

4 rows Color A

6 rows Color B

6 rows Color A

Repeat from * once; then work:

2 rows Color C

4 rows Color A

2 rows Color C

5 rows Color A

At end of last row, ch 1, turn.

Last Row: Continuing with Color A, dec 1 sc over first 2 dc; sc in next 10 dc; * 3 sc in next dc, sc in next 10 dc; dec 2 sc over next 3 dc, sc in next 10 dc; rep from * 5 more times; 3 sc in next sc, sc in next 10 dc, dec 2 sc over last 2 sts.

Finish off. Weave in all yarn ends.

Rippling Shells

Using a large crochet hook, these pretty shells will grow quickly under your flying fingers. Need a gift in a hurry? Then this is an afghan to choose. Try it also in a solid color. We used a brushed mohair type yarn, but it would be just as lovely in a smooth surface yarn.

Rippling Shells

Size
40" x 54"

Materials
Mohair type worsted weight yarn:
12 oz gold (Color A)
12 oz yellow (Color B)
12 oz vanilla (Color C)
12 oz cinnamon (Color D)

Size L (8 mm) crochet hook (or size required for gauge)

Gauge
4 shells = 9"
4 pattern rows = 2"

Notes

1. To change color at end of row, work across row, YO, draw up a lp in last st (3 lps on hook); YO, draw through 2 lps; change to new color, YO, draw through remaining 2 lps.

2. When joining a new color, leave an 8" yarn end to be used later in fringe.

Instructions

With Color A, chain 148 loosely; afghan is worked lengthwise.

Row 1: 2 dc in 4th ch from hook, * skip 2 ch, 1 sc in next ch, skip 2 ch, 5 dc in next ch (shell made); rep from * ending 3 dc in last ch; ch 1, turn.

Row 2: 1 sc in first dc, * 5 dc in next sc, 1 sc in center dc of next shell; rep from * ending 1 sc in top of turning ch; ch 3, turn.

Row 3: 2 dc in first sc, * 1 sc in center dc of next shell, 5 dc in next sc; rep from * ending 3 dc in last sc; ch 1, turn.

Row 4: Rep Row 2; join Color B in last st.

Finish off A, ch 3, turn.

Rows 5-8: With Color B, rep Rows 3 and 2 for 4 rows, changing to Color C on last stitch of Row 8; ch 3, turn.

Rows 9-12: With Color C, rep Rows 3 and 2 for 4 rows, changing to color D on last stitch of Row 12; ch 3, turn.

Rows 13-16: With Color D, rep Rows 3 and 2 for 4 rows, changing to Color A on last stitch of Row 16; ch 3, turn.

Rep Rows 1-16, 4 times. With Color A, rep Rows 1-4 once.

Weave in all loose ends other than the ends reserved for fringe.

Fringe

Follow Single Knot Fringe Instructions on page 140. Cut 50 strands of colors B, C & D and 60 strands of Color A, each 16" long. Fold each strand in half for each knot, tie knot through each row of matching color across each short end of afghan. Five knots are worked in each color segment. Include the extra yarn ends into that particular colored knot.

*P*retty as a plum tree blooming in spring, this afghan will warm your heart on chilly days.

Plum Pretty

Size

45" x 54"

Materials

Worsted weight yarn:
6 oz navy
36 oz print

(Photographed model made with TLC®
Amoré™ Colors #3851 Navy and #3934
Plum Print)

Size H (5 mm) crochet hook, or size
required for gauge

Gauge

10 sts = 3"

Instructions

With navy, ch 141.

Row 1: Sc in 2nd ch from hook and in each
rem ch: 140 sc, ch 1, turn.

Row 2: Sc in each sc, ch 1. turn.

Rows 3 through 12: Rep Row 2; at end of
Row 12, change to plum print in last st, ch
3 (counts as first st of next row), turn.

Row 13 (right side): * Sk next sc, dc in
next sc, dc in skipped sc; rep from * across,
ending dc in last sc; ch 1, turn.

Row 14: Sc in each st, ch 3 turn.

Repeat Rows 13 and 14 in sequence until
piece measures about 50" long, ending by
working Row 13. At end of last row,
change to navy in last st, ch 1, turn.

Work 12 rows in sc, finish off.

Weave in ends.

Summer Skies

*S*oft as a blue summer sky is this easy afghan, worked up quickly on a big crochet hook Size M. Bulky yarn makes it double quick to crochet.

Size
42" x 54" before fringing

Materials
Bulky-weight yarn:
18 oz white (Color A)
12 oz blue (Color B)

(Photographed model made with Lion Brand Homespun® Colors #300 Hepple-white (A) and #329 Waterfall (B))

Size M (9 mm) crochet hook (or size required for gauge)

Gauge
2 dc = 1"

Notes

1. To change color at end of rows: work across, YO, draw up a loop in last st (3 loops on hook), YO, draw through 2 loops, change to new color, YO, draw through remaining 2 loops; ch 2, turn.

2. Ch 2 at end of each row counts as first dc of next row.

continued on the next page

Summer Skies

Pattern Rows

There are two pattern rows; which are worked as follows:

Double Crochet Rows: Sk first dc, dc in next dc and in each dc across; dc under ch-2; ch 2, turn.

Cross Stitch Rows: Sk first dc, dc in next dc; * sk next dc, dc in next dc, dc in skipped dc (cross stitch made); rep from * across; ending dc in last dc, dc under ch-2; you should have 39 cross stitches with 2 dc at each end; ch 2, turn.

Instructions

With Color B, loosely ch 84 sts.

Foundation Row: Dc in 4th ch from hook and in each ch across: 82 dc (counting beg skipped chs as a dc); ch 2, turn.

Work in the following color and row sequence:

With Color B:
* 2 rows Double Crochet

1 row Cross Stitch

4 rows Double Crochet

1 row Cross Stitch

1 row Double Crochet *

Repeat from * to * once more

With Color A: 3 rows Double Crochet

With Color B: 1 row Cross Stitch

With Color A: 4 rows Double Crochet

With Color B: 1 row Cross Stitch

With Color A: 3 rows Double Crochet

With Color B: 1 row Cross Stitch

With Color A: 4 rows Double Crochet

Afghan is now half completed. For second half, work the pattern and color sequence in reverse:

With Color B: 1 row Cross Stitch

With Color A: 3 rows Double Crochet

With Color B: 1 row Cross Stitch

With Color A: 4 rows Double Crochet

With Color B: 1 row Cross Stitch

With Color A: 3 rows Double Crochet

With Color B: 1 row Double Crochet

1 row Cross Stitch

4 rows Double Crochet

1 row Cross Stitch

3 rows Double Crochet

1 row Cross Stitch

4 rows Double Crochet

1 row Cross Stitch

3 rows Double Crochet

Finish off, weave in all loose ends.

Fringe

Follow Single Knot Fringe Instructions on page 140. Cut 168 strands, 16" long in each color. Use 4 strands of White folded in half, for each knot and tie knot through every fourth stitch across each short end of afghan. With Blue, tie knots in between the White knots (knots are now tied into every other stitch).

Beautiful Bobbles

*B*obbles are fun to do and work up quickly, giving a lovely textured effect. The beautiful, soft yarn makes the afghan drape gracefully.

Size
42" x 50" before fringing

Materials
Worsted weight yarn:
36 oz wheat

(Photographed model made with TLC® Amoré™ Color #3220 Wheat)

Size K (6.5 mm) crochet hook (or size required for gauge)

Gauge
6 dc = 2 1/2"
4 pattern rows = 2 1/2"

continued on the next page

Beautiful Bobbles

Instructions

Chain 128 sts loosely; afghan is worked lengthwise.

Foundation Row: Dc in 3rd chain from hook and in each ch across: 126 dc counting beg ch-2 as a dc; ch 1, turn.

Row 1 (wrong side): Sc in first dc, skip next dc, * sc in next dc; (YO and draw up a lp in same dc where last sc was made) 3 times, YO and draw through 6 lps, YO and draw through remaining 2 lps (Bobble made); skip next dc and push Bobble to back. Rep from * to last dc and ch-2, make sc and Bobble in next dc, dc in top of ch-2: 62 Bobbles made; ch 1, turn.

Row 2: Sc in first dc, skip next Bobble; * in next sc, make sc and Bobble, skip next Bobble and push Bobble to the front. Rep from * to last sc, dc in last sc, ch 2, turn.

Row 3: Dc in next Bobble and in each st across, ch 2, turn.

Row 4: Dc in each dc and in top of ch-2; ch 1, turn.

Rep rows 1-4 until afghan measures approx 42", ending by working Row 4. Fasten off. Weave in all loose ends.

Fringe

Follow Single Knot Fringe Instructions on page 140. Cut strands 16" long. Use 4 strands, folded in half, and tie knot around the ch-2 of the 2 Bobble rows across each short end of afghan, plus a knot at the beg and ending dc rows (34 knots each side).

Sweet Cream

This creamy afghan is made up of panels in an easy lace pattern, separated by garter stitch rows which add texture. Pretty braided fringe adds a nice accent. Knitted on a large needle, it is an easy and quick project.

Sweet Cream

Size
41" x 53" before fringing

Materials
Worsted weight yarn:
21 oz cream

(Photographed model made with Lion Brand Wool-Ease® Color #099 Fisherman)

36" size 10 1/2 (6.5 mm) circular needle (or size required for gauge)

14 stitch markers

Gauge
In Lace Pattern: 16 sts = 4 1/2 "

Notes

1. Circular needle is used to accommodate large number of stitches; do not join, work back and forth in rows.

2. For ease in establishing the lace and garter stitch panels, place markers as indicated on the first row. Slip markers as you work each following row. Markers may be removed when pattern is clearly established.

Instructions
Cast on 152 sts; knit 2 rows for border

Row 1: K 8, place marker; * K 2 tog, K 2; YO, K 5, YO; K 2, sl 1 as to knit, K 1, PSSO; K 3, place marker, K 4, place marker. Rep from * to last 8 sts, place marker, K 8.

Row 2: K 8, slip marker, * P 16, slip marker, K 4. Rep from * to last marker, K 8.

Continue to slip markers on following rows.

Row 3: K 8; * K 5, K 2 tog, K 2; YO, K 1, YO, K 2; sl 1, K 1, PSSO, K 2, K 4. Rep from * to last marker, K 8.

Row 4: Rep Row 2.

Row 5: K 8; * K 4, K 2 tog; K 2, YO; K 3, YO, K 2; sl 1, K 1, PSSO, K 1, K 4. Rep from * to last marker, K 8.

Row 6: Rep Row 2.

Row 7: K 8; * K 3, K 2 tog; K 2, YO; K 5, YO, K 2; sl 1, K 1, PSSO; K 4. Rep from * to last marker, K 8.

Row 8: Rep Row 2.

Row 9: K 8; * K 2, K 2 tog, K 2; YO, K 1, YO, K 2; sl 1, K 1, PSSO, K 5, K 4. Rep from * to last marker, K 8.

Row 10: Rep Row 2.

Row 11: K 8, * K 1, K 2 tog, K 2; YO, K 3, YO, K 2; sl 1, K 1, PSSO; K 8. Rep from * to last marker, K 8.

Row 12: Rep Row 2.

Repeat these 12 rows for pattern. Work until piece measures about 53", ending by working Row 11.

Knit 2 more rows. Bind off loosely in knit.

Fringe

Follow Single Knot Fringe Instructions on page 140. Cut strands 16" long and use 2 strands folded in half for each knot. Tie knot through each stitch across each short end of afghan.

Braid yarn from first 3 knots together loosely, knot firmly to fasten, leaving 1" ends. Continue braiding across. Trim ends.

Diagonal Chevrons

*H*ere's an afghan with a plus—it makes its own fringe as you work each row! To create the interesting textured pattern, double crochet stitches are worked in a slanting direction.

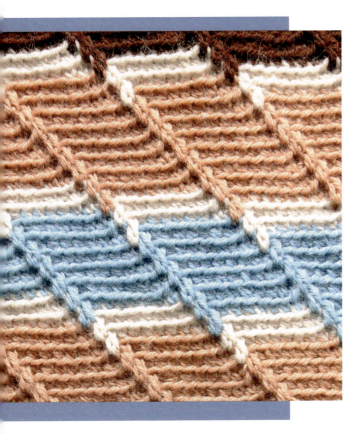

Size

42" x 50"

Materials

Worsted weight yarn:

12 oz heather (Color A)

7 oz blue (Color B)

10 oz brown (Color C)

14 oz tan (Color D)

3 1/2 oz pale blue (Color E)

(Photographed model was made with Lion Brand Wool-Ease® Colors #098 Natural Heather (A), #107 Blue Heather (B), #126 Chocolate Brown (C), #124 Caramel (D), and #116 Delft (E))

Size J (6 mm) crochet hook (or size required for gauge)

Gauge

11 sc = 3"

continued on the next page

Diagonal Chevrons

Notes

To make the fringe as you work, leave a 7" end of yarn at the beginning and end of each row. The afghan is worked from the front side (except where noted) so be sure never to turn the work. Here are some techniques you will want to refer to as you work:

1. All sc stitches are worked in the back lp only of each stitch. This is the lp away from you.

2. All dc stitches are worked in the front lp of the sc stitch in the second row below.

3. From Row 2 on, begin every row like this: Leave a 7" end of yarn, make a slip knot on hook; remove hook, insert it in first st of previous row, put slip knot back on hook and pull lp through, ch 1. This counts as first st of the row. This method gives a firm selvage edge.

4. To end each row, after working last st, cut yarn 7" from hook, pull yarn end through lp. Remember that each row is worked from the front; and that the yarn is joined and ended anew each row.

Color Sequence

Work following pattern in this color sequence:

* 2 rows Color A

4 rows Color B

2 rows Color A

6 rows Color C

2 rows Color A

8 rows Color D

2 rows Color A

6 rows Color E

2 rows Color A

8 rows Color D

2 rows Color A

6 rows Color C

2 rows Color A

4 rows Color B

Rep Color Sequence from * 3 times, then work 2 more rows in Color A.

Color sequence is not mentioned in pattern; be sure to make the color changes as before.

Instructions

With Color A, make a slip knot on hook, leaving a 7" end; ch 186 loosely; afghan is worked lengthwise.

Row 1: Sc in 2nd from hook and in each ch across: 185 sc; finish off, leaving a 7" end.

Rows 2 and 3: Join yarn in first st (Note 3 above); sc in back lp only of each st across; finish off yarn (Note 4 above). Joining and ending methods will not be mentioned again. Be sure to make color changes as you work, and to work in back lp only of each sc.

Row 4: Join yarn in first sc, sc in next sc; sk next sc, work dc in front lp of sc 2 rows below; * sc in next 9 sc, sk next sc, dc as before in 2nd row below; rep from * across, ending with 2 sc.

Row 5: Join yarn in first sc, sc in next 2 sc, sk 1 sc, dc as before; * work 9 sc, dc as before; rep from * across, ending with 1 sc.

Rows 6-13: Rep Row 5, but work one more sc at beginning of each row before working the first dc. This moves all the dc stitches over one space on each row, placing them on a diagonal.

Row 14: Rep Row 4.

Row 15: Rep Row 5.

Rows 16-23: Rep Rows 6-13.

Row 24: Rep Row 4.

Rep these 24 rows for pattern (working Row 1 now into back loop of sc sts instead of into starting chains), following the color sequence.

Edging

At end, with right side of afghan facing, and working over last row completed, join Color A and work 1 row of sc in each stitch across that end of afghan. Fasten off. With right side of afghan facing and working over starting chain, join Color A and sc in each ch across. Fasten off. Trim fringe evenly.

Perfect Plaid

*H*ere's another quickest-of-the-quick! First you make a crochet mesh background then crochet a chain of doubled yarn through the mesh to create the plaid effect. Fun, fast, and easy!

Size

38" x 57" before fringing

Materials

Worsted weight yarn:
16 oz rose
16 oz plum
16 oz green

(Photographed model was with TLC® Amoré™ Colors #3710 Rose, #3534 Plum, and #3625 Celery)

Size J (6 mm) crochet hook (or size required for gauge)

Size K (6.5 mm) crochet hook for weaving

Gauge

For background, 5 (dc, ch1) mesh = 3"
6 rows = 4"

continued on the next page

Perfect Plaid

Instructions
Background
With plum and size J hook, ch 138 loosely.

Foundation Row (right side): Dc in 6th ch from hook; * ch 1, skip 1 ch, dc in next ch; rep from * across: 66 ch-1 sps. Ch 4 (counts as a dc and ch-1 sp), turn.

Pattern Row: Skip first dc and ch-1 sp; * dc in next dc, ch 1, sk ch-1 sp; rep from *, ending dc in 3rd ch of turning ch. Work two more Pattern Rows in plum.

Continue to rep Pattern Row in following color sequence: 2 rows green, 4 rows plum, until piece measures about 57" long. Finish off, weave in all yarn ends.

Vertical Stripes
Now watch your afghan magically turn into a plaid as you weave yarn through the mesh spaces. These vertical (lengthwise) stripes are worked with the size K crochet hook, and two strands of yarn.

Start with right side of work facing you. With plum, make a slip knot on K hook using 2 strands of yarn, and leaving about 8" of yarn ends before the knot to be used as fringe.

Keeping yarn beneath work, begin at lower edge (along foundation chain) of first vertical row of ch-1 spaces and work a sl st in each ch-1 space to top of afghan. To work sl st: Insert hook in ch-1 sp from front to back, hook 2 strands of yarn from beneath work and draw through work and loop on hook: sl st made.

Be sure to work sl sts very loosely so as not to pucker or distort afghan. Finish off, leaving 8" yarn ends as fringe. Again with plum, weave in next vertical row.

Continue weaving in this manner across afghan, using this color sequence:

*1 row green

4 rows rose

1 row green

2 rows plum

Rep color sequence from * across afghan.

Trim fringe evenly.

Sedona Rocks

The beautiful colors of the yarns used in this afghan remind us of the magnificent colored rock formations around Sedona, Arizona. And the afghan would make a perfect cover for a cool Arizona evening.

Sedona Rocks

Size

40" x 54"

Materials

Worsted weight yarn:
12 oz ombre (Color A)
18 oz cinnamon (Color B)

36" size 10¹/₂ (6.5 mm) circular needle
(or size required for gauge)

Two stitch markers

Safety pin

Gauge

In Garter Stitch (knit every row)
3 sts = 1"

Note

There is a Garter Stitch border of 6 sts
on each side of the afghan. Markers are
used to set off these stitches; move
markers on each row.

Instructions

With Color A, cast on 120 sts; do not join,
work back and forth in rows. Knit 12 rows.
Mark last row with safety pin to indicate
wrong side of afghan. Finish off Color A,
join Color B.

Pattern Rows

Row 1: K 6, place marker on right needle;
knit across to last 6 sts, place marker on
right needle, K 6.

Row 2: K 6, sl marker; purl across to marker, sl marker, K 6.

Note

Sl markers on every following row; this will not be mentioned again.

Row 3 (right side): K 6, purl to last 6 sts, K 6.

Row 4: K 6; * K 1; (K 1, P 1, K 1) all in next st; rep from * across to last 6 sts, K 6.

Row 5: K 6; * K 3, P 1; rep from * across to last 6 sts, K 6.

Row 6: K 6; * K 1, P 3 tog; rep from * across to last 6 sts, K 6.

Row 7: K 6; purl to last 6 sts, K 6.

Row 8: K 6; * (K 1, P 1, K 1) all in next st, K 1; rep from * to last 6 sts, K 6.

Row 9: K 6; * P 1, K 3; rep from * across to last 6 sts, K 6.

Row 10: K 6; * P 3 tog, K 1; rep from * across to last 6 sts, K 6.

Rows 11-14: Rep Rows 3-6, ending on right side. Finish off Color B, join Color A.

With Color A, knit 12 rows; change to Color B.

With Color B, work Pattern Rows 1-14; change to Color A.

With Color A, knit 18 rows; change to Color B.

With Color B, work Pattern Rows 1-10; change to Color A.

With Color A, knit 18 rows; change to Color B.

With Color B, work Pattern Rows 1-14; change to Color A.

With Color A, knit 12 rows; change to Color B.

With Color B, work Pattern Rows 1-14; change to Color A.

With Color A, knit 12 rows.

Finish off, weave in ends.

Just for Fun

A bright and cheerful combination of colors makes this afghan one a child will love.

Size
34" x 40"

Materials
Worsted weight yarn:

11 oz white

7 oz green

7 oz lilac

7 oz ombre

(Photographed model made with Bernat®
Berella® "4"® Colors #08942 White,
#01235 Soft Green, #01317 Lilac, and
#09301 Spring Meadow Ombre)

Size K (6.5 mm) crochet hook (or size
required for gauge)

Gauge
3 dc = 1"

4 rows = 3"

continued on the next page

Just for Fun

Instructions

With white, loosely ch 99.

Row 1: Dc in 4th ch from hook and in next ch, (dc, ch 2, dc) in next ch; * dc in next ch, dec over next 3 chs as follows: (YO, draw up a lp in next ch, YO and draw through 2 lps on hook) 3 times, YO and draw through all 4 lps on hook: dec made; dc in next ch, (dc, ch 2, dc) in next ch; rep from * to last 3 chs, dc in next ch, dec over last 2 chs as follows: (YO, draw up a lp in next ch, YO and draw through 2 lps on hook) twice, YO and draw through all 3 lps on hook: dec made; ch 3 (counts as first dc of following row), turn.

Row 2: Dc in each of next 2 dc; * (dc, ch 2, dc) in next ch-2 sp, dc in next dc, dec over next 3 sts, dc in next dc; rep from * to last ch-2 sp, (dc, ch 2, dc) in ch-2 sp, dc in next dc, dec over next 2 dc, leave ch-3 at end of row unworked; ch 3, turn.

Rep Row 2 four times more. At end of last row, change to green in last st (pull new color through last 3 lps), cut white.

Rep Row 2 in the following color sequence:

6 rows green (just joined)

6 rows ombre

6 rows lilac

6 rows white

6 rows green

6 rows ombre

6 rows lilac

6 rows white

At end of last row, finish off and weave in all ends.

Fisherman Cables and Lattice

Two kinds of cables as well as a beautiful lattice pattern make this afghan fun as well as quick to make. Knit it on big needles.

Fisherman Cables and Lattice

Size

50" x 66" before fringing

Materials

Worsted weight yarn:
36 oz off-white

(Photographed model made with TLC® Essentials™ Color #2313 Aran)

36" size 11 (8 mm) circular needle (or size required for gauge)

Cable stitch holder or double-point needle

Two stitch markers

Gauge

4 sts (in stockinette st) = 1"

Instructions

Side Panel (make 2)

Starting at narrow edge, cast on 64 sts loosely; do not join, work back and forth in rows.

Row 1: P 2, K 6, P 2, place a marker on needle; K 44, place a marker on needle; P 2, K 6, P 2.

Row 2: K 2, P 6, K 2, slip marker; purl to next marker slip marker; K 2, P 6, K 2. Slip markers on all following rows.

Row 3: P 2, K 6, P 2;* skip next st; with yarn in front of left needle tip; knit in front of next st but do not slip off needle, knit the skipped st; slip both sts off left needle: Right Twist made; skip next st; knit in back of next st; knit the skipped st. Slip both sts off left needle: Left Twist made. Rep from * to next marker, P 2, K 6, P 2.

Row 4: Rep Row 2.

Row 5: P 2, slip next 3 sts onto dp needle and hold in front of work, K next 3 sts, K the 3 sts from dp needle: Cable Twist made; P 2, * make a Left Twist, make a Right Twist; rep from * to next marker, P 2, Cable Twist as before, P 2.

Row 6: Rep Row 2.

Rep Rows 3–6 for pattern.

Work in pattern until length is 66 inches, ending by working a wrong-side row. Bind off loosely.

Center Panel

Starting at narrow edge, cast on 72 sts. Do not join; work back and forth in rows.

Row 1: P 3, K 6; (P 4, K 6) 6 times; P 3.

Row 2: K 3, P 6; * K 4, P 6. Rep from * to last 3 sts, K3.

Row 3: P 3, slip next 3 sts onto dp or cable needle and hold in back of work, K next 3 sts, K the 3 sts from dp needle: Right Cable Twist made; (P 4, Right Cable Twist) 6 times, P 3.

Row 4: Repeat Row 2.

Row 5: P 2, * slip next st onto dp needle and hold in back of work, K next 3 sts, P the st from dp needle: cable moved to the right; slip next 3 sts onto dp needle and hold in front of work, P next st, K the 3 sts from dp needle: cable moved to the left; P 2; rep from * across.

Row 6: K 2, * P 3, K 2; rep from * across.

Row 7: P 1, * move cable to right, P 2, move cable to left; rep from * to last st, P 1,

Row 8: K 1, P 3, K 4, * P 6, K 4; Repeat from * to last 4 sts, P 3, K 1.

continued on the next page

Fisherman Cables and Lattice

Row 9: P 1, K 3, P 4, slip next 3 sts onto dp needle and hold in front of work, K next 3 sts. K the 3 sts from dp needle:Left Cable Twist made; (P 4, Left Cable Twist) 5 times; P 4, K 3, P 1 .

Row 10: Rep Row 8.

Row 11: P 1, *move cable to left, P 2, move cable to right; rep from * to last st, P 1.

Row 12: Rep Row 6.

Row 13: P 2, move cable to left; * move cable to right, P 2, move cable to left; rep from * to last 6 sts, move cable to right, P 2.

Row 14: Rep. Row 2.

Rep Rows 3-14 for pattern.

Work in pattern until length is same as side panel, ending by working a wrong-side row; bind off loosely.

Finishing

Sew panels together lengthwise, taking care to match rows. For fringe, follow Double Knot Fringe instructions on page 141. Cut strands each 26" long, and use 6 strands in each knot. On each narrow edge of afghan, for Row 1 of fringe, make a knot at corner of each end; then make 49 more knots evenly spaced along same edge. Finish fringe as in instructions.

Horseshoe Cables

Although it looks elaborate, this fisherman afghan is a quick one to knit. Between the unusual Horseshoe Cables are panels of Cellular Stitch, adding interesting texture.

Horseshoe Cables

Size
48" x 52"

Materials
Worsted weight yarn:
24 oz sand

(Photographed model made with TLC®
Amoré™ Color #3005 Sand)

36" size 15 (10 mm) circular needle
(or size required for gauge)

Cable stitch holder or double-point
needle

8 stitch markers

Gauge
In Stockinette Stitch, 12 sts = 5"

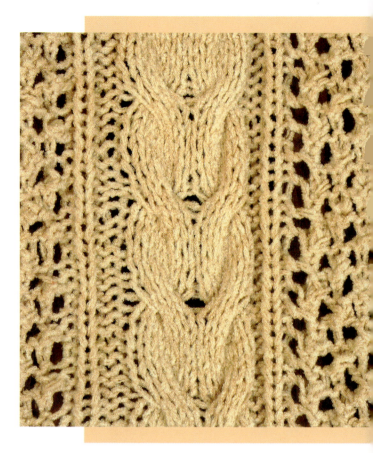

Instructions
With 2 strands held together cast on 120
sts. Do not join, work back and forth in
rows.

Row 1 (wrong side): YO, sl 1, K 2 tog, PSSO; (YO, K 1, YO, sl 1, K 2 tog, PSSO) 6 times; YO, K 1, YO: Cellular Panel made; * place a marker on needle, P 1, place another marker on needle, K 2, P 12, K 2: Horseshoe Panel made; place a marker; P 1, place another marker; YO, sl 1, K 2 tog, PSSO; (YO, K 1,YO, sl 1, K 2 tog, PSSO) 6 times; YO, K 1, YO. Rep from * once more: 123 sts.

Note

Be careful not to drop the YO at beg or end of row; each YO is worked as a st. Three Cellular Panels and two Horseshoe Panels have been started.

Row 2: * Purl to next marker, slip marker K 1, slip marker, P 2, K 12, P 2, slip marker, K 1, slip marker; rep from * once more; purl rem sts. Remember to slip markers on all following rows.

Row 3: YO, K 2 tog; (YO, sl 1, K 2 tog, PSSO; YO, K 1) 6 times; YO, sl 1, K 2 tog, PSSO; * P 1, K 2, P 12, K 2, P 1, YO, K 2 tog; (YO, sl 1, K 2 tog, PSSO, YO, K 1) 6 times; YO, sl 1, K 2 tog, PSSO; rep from * once more: 120 sts.

Row 4: Rep Row 2.

Row 5: YO, sl 1, K 2 tog, PSSO; (YO, K 1, YO, sl 1, K 2 tog, PSSO) 6 times; YO, K1, YO, * P 1, K 2, P 12, K 2, P 1, YO, sl 1, K 2 tog, PSSO; (YO, K 1, YO, sl 1, K 2 tog, PSSO) 6 times; YO, K 1, YO; rep from * once more: 123 sts.

Row 6 (Cable Twist Row): * Purl to next marker, K 1, P 2; slip next 3 sts onto dp needle and hold in back of work; K next 3 sts, K the 3 sts from dp needle, slip next 3 sts onto dp needle and hold in front of work; K next 3 sts, K the 3 sts from dp needle, P 2, K 1; repeat from * once more, purl remaining sts.

Row 7: Rep Row 3.

Row 8: Rep Row 2.

Row 9: Rep Row 5.

Rep Rows 2-9 for pattern. Work in pattern until afghan measures about 52", ending by working a Row 9. Bind off. Weave in ends.

Fringe

Follow Triple Knot Fringe instructions on page 141. Cut the strands each 26" long and use 8 strands in each knot.

*D*eep in the ocean the coral reefs create a place for sealife to hide. This lovely afghan reflects the color of these precious habitats.

Coral Seas Throw

Size
34" x 56"

Materials
Bulky weight yarn:
28 oz coral

(Photographed model made with Lion Brand Homespun® Color #370 Coral Gables)

Size N (10 mm) crochet hook or size required for gauge

Gauge
11 dc = 5"

Instructions
Ch 122.

Row 1: Sc in 2nd ch from hook and in each rem ch: 121 sc; ch 3 (counts as first dc of following row), turn; afghan is worked lengthwise.

Row 2: Dc in each sc, ch 3, turn.

Row 3: Dc in each dc, ch 3, turn.

Rep Row 3 until piece measures 34" long. At end of last row, ch 1, turn.

Last row: Sc in each dc, finish off.

Fringe
Work across each short side edge of afghan as follows: On right side of work, attach yarn at corner, sc in first sc row, *ch 10, sc over post of end dc on next row, ch 5, sc over post of next dc; rep from * across side edge, ending with sc in last sc row. Finish off.

Mock Fisherman

Size

42" x 55" before fringing

Materials

Worsted weight yarn:
20 oz off-white

(Photographed model made with Caron® One Pound, Color #589 Cream)

36" Size 11 (8 mm) circular needle (or size required for gauge)

Gauge

In Garter St (knit every row) 7 sts = 2"

Notes

In the following Mock Cable pattern, there are two special techniques.

1. In Row 1 of the pattern, you will be told to: sl 1, K 2, PSSO the two knit stitches. To do this, first be sure the yarn is moved back to the position for knitting before you slip the stitch. To PSSO, insert tip of left needle into the slipped stitch, draw it over the two knitted stitches, over and off the top of the right-hand needle This results in one stitch decreased.

2. In Row 2 of the pattern, you will be told to: P 1, YO, P 1. To work this YO, bring the yarn back over the needle and completely around it to the front to again have yarn in the purl position. This results in one stitch increased.

If you've always wanted to make a beautiful fisherman knit afghan but were afraid to tackle all those elaborate cable stitches, this is the project for you! The pattern is an easy mock cable with only four rows, which works up quickly on size 11 needles. A rich fringe provides the finishing touch.

continued on the next page

Mock Fisherman

Mock Cable Pattern

Row 1 (right side): K 5, P 2; * sl 1, K 2, PSSO the two knit stitches; P 2; rep from * to last 5 sts, K 5.

Row 2: K 7; * P 1; YO, P 1, K 2; rep from * to last 5 sts, K 5.

Row 3: K 5, P 2; * K 3 (work the YO of previous row as a st), P 2; rep from * to last 5 sts, K 5.

Row 4: K 7, * P 3, K 2; rep from * to last 5 sts, K 5. Rep Rows 1 through 4 for pattern.

Instructions

Loosely cast on 157 sts; do not join, work back and forth in rows.

Bottom Border: Knit 2 rows. Now rep Rows 1 through 4 of Mock Cable pattern until piece measures 54" long, ending by working Row 4 of pattern.

Top Border: Knit 2 rows. Bind off loosely. Weave in ends.

Fringe

Follow Triple Knot Fringe instructions on page 141. Cut strands 22" long, and use 10 strands, folded in half, for each knot. Hold afghan with right side facing and one short edge at top. Working from left to right, make first knot in outer edge st of garter st side border, second knot in inner st of garter st side border, then work one knot below each cable across to other side. Work one knot in inner st of garter st side border, last knot in outer st of garter st side border.

Blue Boy

Textured seed stitch panels combined with chevrons make the interesting design for this afghan. It would be just as pretty in yellow, pink, lavender or white.

Blue Boy

Size

33" x 38" before fringing

Materials

Bulky weight yarn:
12 oz

(Photographed model made with Lion Brand Jiffy® Color #1066 Baby Blue)

29" size 15 (10 mm) circular needle (or size required for gauge)

8 stitch markers

Gauge

In Stockinette Stitch (K 1 row, P 1 row), 5 sts = 2"

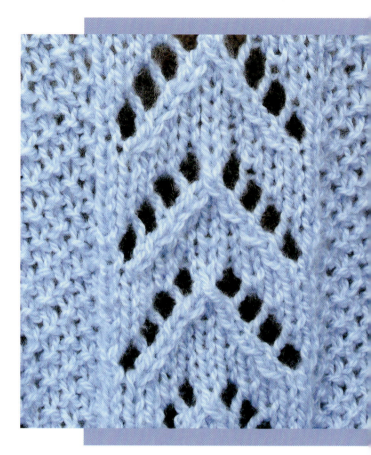

Note

Markers are used to separate the Seed Stitch patterns from the Chevron Patterns for ease in working; sl markers on every row.

Stitch Patterns

Seed Stitch Pattern (worked over 7 sts): (K 1, P 1) 3 times; K 1.

Chevron Panel Pattern (worked over 11 sts):
Rows 1, 3, 5, 7: Purl (wrong side).

Row 2: K 1, YO, Sl 1, K 1, PSSO, K 5, K 2 tog, YO, K 1.

Row 4: K 2, YO, Sl 1, K 1, PSSO, K 3, K 2 tog, YO, K 2.

Row 6: K 3, YO, Sl 1, K 1, PSSO, K 1, K 2 tog, YO, K 3.

Row 8: K 4, YO, Sl 1, K 2 tog, PSSO, YO, K 4.

Instructions

Cast on 79 sts; do not join; work back and forth in rows.

Row 1 (wrong side): Work in Seed St for 7 sts, * place marker on right needle; P 11 (Chevron Panel), place marker on right needle; work Seed St for 7 sts; rep from * across.

Row 2: Work in Seed St to first marker; * move marker to right needle, work Row 2 of Chevron pattern, move marker work in Seed St to next marker; rep from * across ending last repeat with seed st on last 7 sts.

Row 3: Rep Row 1 moving markers.

Row 4: Rep Row 2, BUT work Row 4 of Chevron Panel pattern.

Row 5: Rep Row 1.

Row 6: Rep Row 2, BUT work Row 6 of Chevron Panel pattern.

Row 7: Rep Row 1.

Row 8: Rep Row 2, BUT work Row 8 of Chevron Panel pattern.

Repeat these 8 rows until afghan measures about 38", ending by working Row 8.

Bind off loosely in pattern stitch.

Fringe

Follow Single Knot Fringe Instructions on page 140. Cut strands 16" long and use two strands doubled for each knot. Tie knot through every other cast-on or bound-off stitch across each short end of afghan.

Gingham and Lace

*A*ny baby will love this sweet gingham wrap, accented with a crisp white lacy ruffle. Make it in pink for a girl, or in any other combination of a medium and light color with white. A simple two-round granny motif creates the gingham effect. It's an easy to make, great to give project.

Size

42" square, including ruffle

Materials

Worsted weight yarn:
8 oz medium blue (Color A)
16 oz lt blue (Color B)
12 oz white (Color C)

Size I (9 mm) aluminum crochet hook
(or size required for gauge)

Gauge

One motif = 2$\frac{1}{2}$"

continued on the next page

Gingham and Lace

Instructions

Granny Motif: make 56 with Color A; 113 with Color B and 56 with Color C.

Rnd 1: Ch 4, join with a sl st to form a ring; ch 3, 2 dc in ring; * ch 2, 3 dc in ring; rep from * twice, ch 2, join with a sl st to top of beg ch-3.

Rnd 2: Sl st in each of next 2 dc and into ch-2 corner sp; ch 3, work (2 dc, ch 2, 3 dc) in same ch-2 sp; * work (3 dc, ch 2, 3 dc) in next ch-2 corner sp; rep from * twice, join with a sl st in top of beg ch-3. Finish off, weave in ends.

Assembling

Afghan has 15 rows, with 15 squares in each row. Every odd-numbered row contains squares as follows, from left to right: * Color A, Color B; rep from * 7 times, end with Color A. Every even-numbered row contains squares as follows, from left to right: * Color C, Color B, rep from * 7 times, end with Color C.

To join, hold 2 squares with right sides together. Carefully matching stitches, begin in ch st at corner and sew with over-cast st in outer lps only, ending in ch st at next corner. Join all motifs for each row, then join rows in same manner.

Ruffle

Rnd 1: Hold afghan with right side facing you; join white with sc in any outer corner ch-3 sp; work 2 more sc in same sp; sc in each st and each joining around, working 3 sc in each outer corner; join with a sl st to first sc.

Rnd 2: Sl st into next sc; ch 4 (counts as a dc and ch-1 sp). In same st work (dc, ch 1, dc,): corner made; * ch 1, sk next sc, dc in next sc; rep from * around, working (dc, ch 1, dc, ch 1, dc) in center sc of each corner sp; end ch 1, join to 3rd ch of beg ch-4.

Rnd 3: Ch 5 (counts as a dc and ch-2), dc in same ch as joining; * sk next ch-1 sp, (dc, ch 2, dc) in next dc; rep from * around, join in 3rd ch of beg ch-5.

Rnd 4: Sl st into next ch-2 sp, (ch 3, dc, ch 2, 2 dc) all in same sp; * (2 dc, ch 2, 2 dc) in next ch-2 sp; rep from * around, join to 3rd ch of beg ch.

Finish off, weave in ends.

Classic Granny

The granny afghan we all know and love was made with scrap yarn, which made the afghan a colorful mix of different yarns. Our version is the classic granny with a twist: we've used ombre shades instead of solids for the centers of the squares. The first three rounds of each square are worked in an ombre; the fourth round in black. The look is bright and cheerful. You may, of course, use scraps for the centers if you prefer.

Classic Granny

Size
47" x 58"

Materials
Worsted weight yarn:
12 oz rose ombre
18 oz purple ombre
12 oz green ombre
18 oz blue ombre
10 1/2 oz black

(Photographed model made with Red Heart® Classic, Colors #973, Berries (rose), #985 Purples, #957 Greens, #960 Blues, and #12 Black)

Size I (5.5 mm) crochet hook (or size required for gauge)

Gauge
1 square = 5 1/2 "

Instructions
Following Square instructions, make 20 rose, 28 blue, 20 green, 12 purple.

Square Instructions
With Ombre, ch 4; join with a sl st to form a ring.

Rnd 1: Ch 3 (counts as 1 dc), 2 dc in ring; * ch 3, 3 dc in ring; rep from * twice more, ch 3; join with a sl st to top of ch-3; sl st to ch-3 space.

Rnd 2: Ch 3, 2 dc in same space; * ch 2, in next space work (3 dc, ch 3, 3 dc); rep from * twice more, ch 2, 3 dc in same space as first ch-3, ch 3, join with sl st to top of ch-3; sl st to next ch-3 space.

Rnd 3: Ch 3, 2 dc in same space; * ch 2, 3 dc in next space, ch 2; in corner space work (3 dc, ch 3, 3 dc); rep from *, ending ch 2, 3 dc in same space as first ch-3, ch 3, join with a sl st to top of ch-3. Fasten off.

Rnd 4: Join Black in any ch-3 sp; rep Rnd 3, having two groups of 3-dc between corners; fasten off. Weave in all ombre yarn ends, but leave the black yarn ends for later.

Joining

Squares are joined into 10 rows of 8 squares each. To join, hold two squares with right sides facing; sl st squares together loosely with black, inserting the hook into the back loops only of each square. Join each row of squares first; tie a number on each finished row so that you don't get them mixed up later when joining row to row. Join squares in each row as follows (from left to right):

Row 1: 8 Rose.

Row 2: 8 Blue.

Row 3: 1 Blue, 6 Green, 1 Blue.

Row 4: 1 Blue, 1 Green, 4 Purple, 1 Green, 1 Blue.

Row 5: 1 Blue, 1 Green, 1 Gold, 2 Rose, 1 Gold, 1 Green, 1 Blue.

Row 6: Same as Row 5.

Row 7: Same as Row 4.

Row 8: Same as Row 3.

Row 9: Same as Row 2.

Row 10: Same as Row 1.

Now join the strips from top (Row 1) to bottom, slip stitching each strip to the one below, again with right sides facing and working into back lp of each stitch; carefully match stitches as you work, and work a ch-1 between each square (this keeps work flat). Weave in all loose black ends, running the ends into the seam of the next square, rather than back into the square itself.

Edging

Join Black with a sl st into any outer corner ch-3 sp; work as for Rnd 3 of square; work one more rnd in Black; finish off, weave in ends.

Dimensional Shells

*S*oft and luscious, this beautiful yarn in a deep blue cries out to be wrapped around you! Everyone who has seen it wants to claim this afghan! The unusual stitch gives a dimensional shell effect.

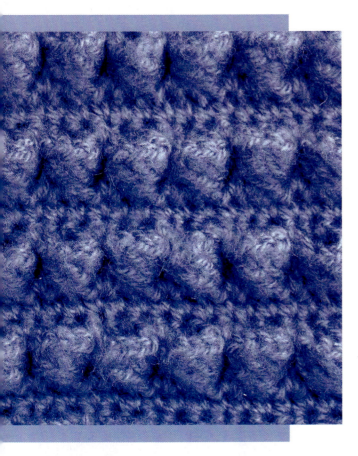

Size
44" x 56"

Materials
Bulky weight yarn:
52 oz blue

(Photographed model made with Lion Brand Jiffy® Color #109 Royal)

Size N (10 mm) crochet hook, or size required for gauge.

Gauge
12 dc = 4"

continued on the next page

Dimensional Shells

Special Shell Stitch

Insert hook from front to back to front around post (vertical bar) of specified dc; work shell of (sc, hdc, 3 dc) around post.

Instructions

Ch 133.

Row 1: Sc in 2nd ch from hook in each rem ch: 132 sc; ch 1, turn.

Row 2: Sc in each sc, ch 3, turn.

Row 3: Dc in each dc, turn

Row 4 (right side): Ch 3 (counts as first dc of row), sc in next dc, work shell around post of same dc; * sk 2 dc, sc in next dc, shell around post of same dc; rep from * across, dc in last dc, ch 1, turn.

Row 5: Sc in each skipped dc and in each sc; ch 1, turn.

Row 6: Sc in each sc, ch 3, turn.

Rep Rows 3 through 6 for pattern, until piece measures about 56", ending by working Row 6. At end of last row, work 3 sc in last sc for corner.

Edging

Rnd 1: Work sc around next long side, bottom, opposite side, and top, working 3 sc in each rem corner and taking care to keep work flat; join to beg sc.

Rnd 2: Sk 2 sc, in next sc work * (sc, hdc, 3 dc); sk 2 sc; rep from * ending sk 2 sc, join in first sc. Finish off.

Weave in ends.

Afghan Basics

HOW TO KNIT

CASTING ON

There are many ways to cast on. If you are a beginner, try this easy method. Use only one needle. First, measure a length of yarn that will give you about 1" for each stitch to be cast on. First make a slip knot on the needle; make a yarn loop, leaving about 4" of yarn at the free end; insert the needle into the loop and draw up the yarn from the free end to make a loop on the needle.

Pull the yarn ends firmly, but not too tightly to form the slip knot on the needle. This slip knot counts as your first stitch.

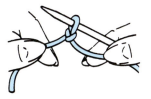

Now begin the casting on:
Step One: Hold the needle with the slip knot in your right hand and with yarn from the skein to your left. With your left hand, make a yarn loop.

Insert the needle into the loop.

Step Two: Still holding the loop in your left hand, with your right hand, pick up the yarn from the skein and bring it back to front around the needle.

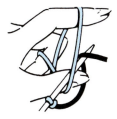

Step Three: Bring the needle through the loop and toward you; at the same time, pull gently on the yarn end to tighten the loop. Make it snug but not tight below the needle.

You have now cast on one stitch. Repeat Steps 1 through 3 for each additional stitch required.

THE KNIT STITCH

Step One: Hold the needle with the cast-on stitches in your left hand. Insert the point of the right needle into the first stitch, from right to left.

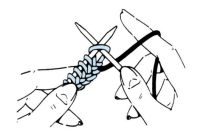

Step Two: With right index finger, bring the yarn under and over the point of the right needle.

Step Three: Draw the yarn through the stitch with the right needle point.

Step Four: Slip the loop on the left needle off, so the new stitch is entirely on the right needle.

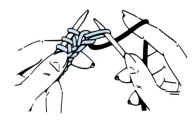

You have now made one complete knit stitch.

THE PURL STITCH

The purl stitch is actually the reverse of the knit stitch. Instead of inserting the right needle point from left to right under the left needle (as you did for the knit stitch), you now insert it from right to left, in front of the left needle.

Afghan Basics

Step One: Insert the right needle from right to left, into the first stitch and in front of the left needle,

Step Two: Holding the yarn in front of the work (side toward you), bring it around the right needle counterclockwise.

Step Three: With right needle, pull the yarn back through the stitch.

Step Four: Slide the stitch off the left needle, leaving the new stitch on the right needle.

You have now made one complete purl stitch.

BINDING OFF

When a piece is finished, you need to get it off the needles. This is called binding off, and here is how to do it.

To bind off on the knit side:

Step One: Knit the first 2 stitches. Now insert the left needle into the first of the 2 stitches.

Draw the first stitch up and over the second stitch and completely off the needle. You have now bound off one stitch.

Step Two: Knit one more stitch; insert left needle into the first stitch on the right needle and draw it up and over the new stitch and completely off the needle. Another stitch is now bound off.

Repeat Step Two until all the stitches are bound off and one loop remains on the right-hand needle. Now to "finish off" or "end off" the yarn, cut it and draw end through the last loop to tighten.

To bind off on the purl side:

Step One: Purl the first 2 stitches. Now insert the left needle into the first stitch on the right needle, and draw it up and over the second stitch and completely off the needle. You have now bound off one stitch.

Step Two: Purl one more stitch; insert the left needle into the first stitch on the right needle and draw it over the new stitch and completely off the needle. Another stitch is bound off.

Repeat Step Two until all stitches are bound off; then finish off.

YARN OVER

To make a yarn over (an extra lp on needle) before a knit stitch:

Bring the yarn to the front of the work as if you were going to purl, then take it over the right needle to the back into the position for knitting; then knit the next stitch.

To make a yarn over before a purl stitch

Bring the yarn around the right needle from front to back over the needle, then to front again under the needle into position for purling; purl the next stitch.

HOW TO CROCHET

CHAIN (CH)

Crochet starts with a basic chain stitch. To begin, make a slip loop on the hook leaving a 4" tail of yarn.

Step 1: Take the hook in the right hand, holding it between the thumb and third finger, and rest the index finger near the tip of the hook.

Step 2: Take the slip loop in the thumb and index finger of the left hand and bring the yarn over the third finger of the left hand, catching it loosely at the left palm with the remaining two fingers.

Step 3: Bring the yarn over the hook from back to front and draw through the loop on the hook.

You have now made one chain stitch. Repeat step 3 for each additional chain desired, moving your thumb and index finger up close to the hook after each stitch or two.

Note: When counting the number of chains, do not count the loop on the hook or the starting slip knot.

SINGLE CROCHET (SC)

First, make a chain to the desired length.

Step 1: Insert the hook in the top loop of the 2nd chain from the hook

Hook the yarn, bringing the yarn over the hook from the back to the front, and draw through.

Step 2: Hook the yarn and draw through 2 loops on the hook.

You have now made one single crochet stitch. To finish the row, work a single crochet (repeat Steps 1 and 2) in each chain.

To work additional rows, chain 1 and turn work counterclockwise. Inserting hook under 2 top loops of the stitch, work a single crochet in each stitch across.

DOUBLE CROCHET (DC)

Begin by making a chain the desired length.

Step 1: Bring the yarn once over the hook; insert the hook in the top loop of the 4th chain from the hook.

Hook the yarn and draw through.

Step 2: Hook yarn and draw through first 2 loops on the hook.

Step 3: Hook yarn again and draw through last 2 loops on hook.

You have now made one double crochet. To finish the row, work a double crochet (repeat Steps 1, 2 and 3) in each chain.

To work additional rows, make 3 chains and turn work counter clockwise. Beginning in 2nd chain (3 chains count as first double crochet).

Work a double crochet in each stitch across, remembering to insert the hook under 2 top loops of the stitch. At the end of the row, work the last double crochet in the top chain of the chain-3.

HALF DOUBLE CROCHET (HDC)

Begin by making a chain the desired length.

Step 1: Bring the yarn over the hook. Insert the hook in the top loop of the 3rd chain from the hook. Hook yarn and draw through (3 loops now on hook).

Step 2: Hook yarn and draw through all 3 loops on the hook.

Afghan Basics

You have now made one half double crochet. To finish the row, work a half double crochet (repeat steps 1 and 2) in each chain.

To work additional rows, make 2 chains and turn work counterclockwise. Beginning in 2nd stitch (2 chains count as first half double crochet), work a half double crochet in each stitch across. At the end of the row, work the last half double crochet in the top chain of the chain-2.

TRIPLE CROCHET (TR)

Begin by making a chain the desired length

Step 1: Bring yarn twice over the hook. Insert the hook in the 5th chain from the hook.

Hook yarn and draw through.

Step 2: Hook yarn and draw through the first 2 loops on the hook.

Step 3: Hook yarn and draw through the next two loops on the hook.

Step 4: Hook yarn and draw through the remaining 2 loops on the hook.

You have now made one triple crochet. To finish the row, work a triple crochet (repeat steps 1 through 4) in each remaining chain.

To work additional rows, make 4 chains and turn work counter clockwise. Beginning in 2nd stitch (4 chains count as first triple crochet), work a triple crochet as before in each chain across. At the end of the row, work the last triple crochet in the top chain of chain-4.

SLIP STITCH (SL ST)

This stitch is used to join work or to move the yarn across a group of stitches without adding any height to the project.

Begin by making a chain the desired length.

Step 1: Insert hook in 2nd chain from hook. Hook yarn and draw through both stitch and loop on hook in one motion.

EDGINGS

SINGLE CROCHET EDGING:

To make this edging, you will be asked to "keep your work flat". This means to adjust your stitches as you work. It may be necessary to skip a row or stitch here or there to keep the edging from rippling; or to add a stitch to keep the work from pulling in, When working around a corner, it is usually necessary to work 3 stitches in the center corner stitch to keep the corner flat and square.

REVERSE SINGLE CROCHET EDGING

This produces a lovely corded effect and is usually worked after a row of single crochet. It is worked on the right side from left to right (the opposite direction for working single crochet).

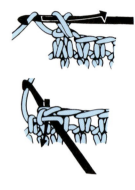

FRINGE

BASIC INSTRUCTIONS

Cut a piece of cardboard about 6" wide and half as long as specified in the instructions for strands, plus $1/2$" for trimming allowance. Wind the yarn loosely and evenly lengthwise around cardboard. When the card is filled, cut the yarn across one end. Do this several times; then begin fringing. You can wind additional strands as you need them.

SINGLE KNOT FRINGE

Hold the specified number of strands for one knot of fringe together, then fold in half.

Hold the knitted project with the right side facing you. Using a crochet hook, draw the folded ends through the space or stitch from right to wrong side.

Pull the loose ends through the folded section.

Draw the knot up firmly.

Space the knots as indicated in the pattern instructions. Trim the ends of the fringe evenly.

DOUBLE KNOT FRINGE

Begin by working Single Knot Fringe. With right side facing you and working from left to right, take half the strands of one knot and half the strands in the knot next to it, and knot them together.

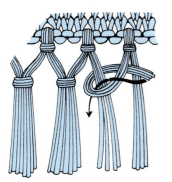

TRIPLE KNOT FRINGE

First work Double Knot Fringe. Then working again on right side from left to right, tie the third row of knots.

ABBREVIATIONS AND SYMBOLS

Knit and crochet patterns are written in a special shorthand, which is used so that instructions don't take up too much space. They sometimes seem confusing, but once you learn them, you'll have no trouble following them.

THESE ARE STANDARD ABBREVIATIONS

Beg . . . . beginning
BO . . . . bind off
CL(s) . . . . cluster
CO. . . . . cast on
Cont . . . . continue
Ch(s) . . . . chain(s)
Dc . . . . double crochet
dec . . . . decrease
Dtr . . . . double triple crochet
Fig . . . . figure
Hdc . . . . half double crochet
inc . . . . increase(ing)
K . . . . knit
Lp(s) . . . . loop(s)
P. . . . . purl
patt . . . . pattern
prev . . . . previous
PSSO . . . . . pass the slipped stitch over

Rem . . . . remain(ing)
Rep . . . . repeat(ing)
Rnd(s) . . . . round(s)
Sc . . . . single crochet
Sk . . . . skip
Sl . . . . slip
Sl st . . . . slip stitch
Sp(s) . . . . space(s)
St(s) . . . . stitch(es)
Stock st . . . . stockinette stitch
Tbl . . . . through back loop
Tog . . . . together
Tr . . . . triple crochet
YO . . . . . yarn over the needle or hook

THESE ARE STANDARD SYMBOLS

* An asterisk (or double asterisks**) in a pattern row, indicates a portion of instructions to be used more than once. For instance, "rep from" three times" means that after working the instructions once, you must work them again three times for a total of 4 times in all.

† A dagger (or double daggers††) indicates those instructions that will be repeated again later in the same row or round.

: The number after a colon tells you the number of stitches you will have when you have completed the row or round.

( ) Parentheses enclose instructions which are to be worked the number of times following the parentheses. For instance, "(ch 1, sc , ch 1) 3 times" means that you will chain one, work one sc, and then chain once again three times for a total of six chains and 3sc.

Parentheses often set off or clarify a group of stitches to be worked into the same space or stitch. For instance, "(dc, ch 2, dc) in corner sp."

[ ] Brackets and ( ) parentheses are also used to give you additional information.

Afghan Basics

TERMS

Front Loop—This is the loop toward you at the top of the stitch

Back Loop—This is the loop away from you at the top of the stitch

Post—This is the vertical part of the stitch

Join—This means to join with a sl st unless another stitch is specified.

Finish Off—This means to end your piece by pulling the yarn through the last loop remaining on the hook. This will prevent the work from unraveling.

Continue in Pattern as Established—This means to follow the pattern stitch as it has been set up, working any increases or decreases in such a way that the pattern remains the same as it was established.

Work Even—This means that the work is continued in the pattern as established without increasing or decreasing.

GAUGE

This is probably the most important aspect of knitting and crocheting!

GAUGE simply means the number of stitches per inch, and the number of rows per inch that result from a specified yarn worked with hooks or needles in a specified size. But since everyone knits or crochets differently—some loosely, some tightly, some in-between—the measurements of individual work can vary greatly, even when the crocheters or knitters use the same pattern and the same size yarn and hook or needle.

If you don't work to the gauge specified in the pattern, your projects will never be the correct size, and you may not have enough yarn to finish your project.

Hook and needle sizes given in instructions are merely guides, and should never be used without a gauge swatch. Crochet or knit a swatch that is about 4" square, using the suggested hook or needle and the number of stitches given in the pattern. Measure your swatch. If the number of stitches are fewer than those listed in the pattern, try making another swatch with a smaller hook or needle. If the number of stitches are more than are called for in the pattern, try making another swatch with a larger hook or needle. It is your responsibility to make sure you achieve the gauge specified in the pattern.

The patterns in this book have been written using the knitting and crochet terminology that is used in the United States. Terms which may have different equivalents in other parts of the world are listed below

United States	International
Double crochet (dc)	treble crochet (tr)
Gauge	tension
Half double crochet (hdc)	half treble crochet
Single crochet (sc)	double crochet (dc)
Skip	miss
Slip stitch (sl st)	single crochet
Triple crochet (tr)	double treble crochet (dtr)
Yarn over (YO)	Yarn forward (yfwd)
Yarn around needle (yrn)	Yarn over hook (yoh)

KNITTING NEEDLES CONVERSION CHART

U.S.	0	1	2	3	4	5	6	7	8	9	10	10½	11	13	15	17
METRIC	2	2.25	2.75	3.25	3.5	3.75	4	4.5	5	5.5	6	6.5	8	9	10	12.75

CROCHET HOOKS CONVERSION CHART

U.S.	B-1	C-2	D-3	E-4	F-5	G-6	H-8	I-9	J-10	K-10½	N	P	Q
METRIC	2.25	2.75	3.25	3.5	3.75	4	5	5.5	6	6.5	9	10	15

Carol Wilson Mansfield, Photography
Graphic Solutions, inc-chgo, Book Design

All of the afghans in this book were
tested to ensure the accuracy and clarity
of the instructions. We are grateful to
the following pattern testers who made
the afghans photographed in this book:

Jana M. Eckman-Borem,
        Tomahawk, Wisconsin
Denise Black, Oceanside, California
Kim Britt, Gurnee, Illinois
Linda Bushey, Anza, California
Sharon Butcher, Valdosta, Georgia
Kathy Christensen,
        Oceanside, California
Carrie Cristiano, Escondido, California
Vinette De Phillipe, Galien, Michigan
Patricia Honaker, East Liverpool, Ohio
Debra Hughes, Lusby, Maryland
Lois Karklus, Tulsa, Oklahoma
Diane La Valle, Brainard, Minnesota
Jodi Lewanda,
        Farmington, Connecticut
Jennie Lute, Kingsville, Ohio
Kelly Robinson, Anza, California
Susie Adams Steele,
        San Marcos, California

Whenever we have used a specialty yarn, we have given the brand name. If you
are unable to find these yarns locally, write to the following manufacturers who
will be able to tell you where to purchase their products, or consult their web
sites. We also wish to thank these companies for supplying yarn for this book:

Bernat Yarns
320 Livingston Avenue South
Listowel, Ontario
Canada N4W 3H3
www.bernat.com

Caron International
Customer Service
P. O. Box 222
Washington, North Carolina 27889
www.caron.com

Lion Brand Yarn Company
34 West 15th Street
New York, New York 10011
www.LionBrand.com

Red Heart Yarns
Coats and Clark
Consumer Services
P. O. Box 12229
Greenville, South Carolina 29612-0229
www.coatsandclark.com

TLC Yarns
Coats and Clark
Consumer Services
P. O. Box 12229
Greenville, South Carolina 29612-0229
www.coatsandclark.com

Every effort has been made to ensure the accuracy of these instructions.
We cannot, however, be responsible for human error or variations in your work.

143

Index

Abbreviations, 141
Baby Afghans
    Blue Boy, 125
    Delightful Daisies, 68
    Gingham and Lace, 128
    Just for Fun, 110
    Lovely Lace, 62
    Peppermint Candy, 45
    Pink Petals, 57
    Raspberries and Cream, 65
    Stripes on Parade, 59
Beautiful Bobbles, Crochet, 94
Beautiful in Blue Cables, Knit, 13
Blue Boy, Knit, 125
Blue Lagoon, Crochet, 42
Blue Rhapsody, Knit, 54
Classic Granny, Crochet, 131
Coral Seas Throws, Crochet, 120
Crocheted Afghans
    Beautiful Bobbles, 94
    Blue Lagoon, 42
    Classic Granny, 131
    Coral Seas Throws, 120
    Delightful Daisies, 68
    Diagonal Chevrons, 100
    Dimensional Shells, 134
    Fantastic Fisherman, 21
    Flower Field Lapghan, 6
    Gingham and Lace, 128
    Ice Crystals, 9
    In the Pink, 50
    Just for Fun, 110
    Marvelous Mauve Lapghan, 39
    Multi-Color Striped, 36
    Ocean Waves, 82
    Peppermint Candy, 45
    Perfect Plaid, 104
    Pink Petals, 57
    Plum Pretty, 88
    Pretty Stripes, 71
    Rippling Shells, 85

Roses in the Snow, 77
Rosy Future, 74
Rosy Ripple, 18
Stripes on Parade, 59
Summer Garden, 30
Summer Skies, 90
Watercolors Afghan, 24
Crochet How To, 138
Delightful Daisies, Crochet, 68
Diagonal Chevrons, Crochet, 100
Dimensional Shells, Crochet, 134
Double Crochet, 139
Double Knot Fringe, 141
Easy Feather and Fan, Knit, 52
Edgings, 140
Fantastic Fisherman, Crochet, 21
Feather and Fan, Knit, 80
Fisherman Cables and Lattice, Knit, 113
Flower Field Lapghan, Crochet, 6
Fringe, 140
Gauge, 142
Gingham and Lace, Crochet, 128
Half Double Crochet, 139
Horseshoe Cables, Knit, 117
Ice Crystals, Crochet, 9
In the Pink, Crochet, 50
Just for Fun, Crochet, 110
Knitted Afghans
    Beautiful in Blue Cables, 13
    Blue Boy, 125
    Blue Rhapsody, 54
    Easy Feather and Fan, 52
    Feather and Fan, 80
    Fisherman Cables and Lattice, 113
    Horseshoe Cables, 117
    Lovely Lace, 62
    Mock Fisherman, 122
    Orchid Lace, 16
    Quick Lace, 33
    Raspberries and Cream, 65
    Raspberry Rose, 27

Sedona Rocks, 107
Sweet Cream, 97
Vanilla Lace Throw, 48
Knitting How To, 137
Lovely Lace, Knit, 62
Marvelous Mauve Lapghan, Crochet, 39
Mock Fisherman, Knit, 122
Multi-Color Striped, Crochet, 36
Ocean Waves, Crochet, 82
Orchid Lace, Knit, 16
Peppermint Candy, Crochet, 45
Perfect Plaid, Crochet, 104
Pink Petals, Crochet, 57
Plum Pretty, Crochet, 88
Pretty Stripes, Crochet. 71
Purl Stitch, 137
Quick Lace, Knit, 33
Raspberries and Cream, Knit, 65
Raspberry Rose, Knit, 27
Reverse Single Crochet Edging, 140
Rippling Shells, Crochet, 85
Roses in the Snow, Crochet, 77
Rosy Future, Crochet, 74
Rosy Ripple, Crochet, 18
Sedona Rocks, Knit, 107
Single Crochet, 139
Single Crochet Edging, 140
Single Knot Fringe, 140
Slip Stitch, 140
Stripes on Parade, Crochet, 59
Summer Garden, Crochet, 30
Summer Skies, Crochet, 90
Sweet Cream, Knit, 97
Symbols, 141
Terms, 142
Triple Crochet, 140
Triple Knot Fringe, 141
Vanilla Lace Throw, Knit, 48
Watercolors Afghan, Crochet, 24